This Chumash workbook is dedicated
in loving memory of

Rabbi Meyer and Mrs. Leya Zanitsky z"l

לזכר ולעילוי נשמת
הרב מרדכי מאיר ב"ר יעקב אליהו זניצקי זצ"ל
נפטר ב' אדר תשנ"ח לפ"ק

וזוגתו אשת חבר אשה צנועה
מרת לאה בת הרב יצחק מרדכי ע"ה
נפטרה כ"ט אדר א' תשס"ה לפ"ק

תנצב"ה

Rabbi Zanitsky was a renowned Torah scholar who used his
extraordinary knowledge of *dikduk* (Hebrew grammar) to teach and
influence thousands of students where he lived in Cleveland, Ohio –
many of whom are among today's leading educators.

Although Rabbi Meyer and Mrs. Leya Zanitsky were childless and were
never able to teach these lessons to their own children, our *chazal* (sages)
inform us that one who teaches Torah to children is considered to be
similar to a parent (Sanhedrin 19a).

With that in mind, we are confident that the Zanitskys will have nachas
in Gan Eden watching many thousands of Hashem's children gain
fluency and a love for Chumash as a result of these pages.

We would like to thank

omni
MANAGED HEALTH

for its corporate sponsorship
of this workbook.

Jerry and Barbara Weissman
of Omni Managed Health
are deeply committed to a wide range of charitable causes
and Bright Beginnings is honored to be included
in their efforts to promote excellence in Jewish education.

Rabbi Yakov Horowitz

Torah Umesorah
תורה ומסורה

The National Society
for Hebrew Day Schools

November 10, 2010

Rabbi Yakov Horowitz
Yeshiva Darchei Noam
257 Grandview Ave.
Suffern, NY 10901

Dear Rabbi Horowitz,

It gives me great pleasure to wish you and your very capable dedicated Staff of Rebbeim at Yeshiva Darchei Noam, a *yasher koach* on making this significant tool available for the world of Torah *chinuch*.

The BRIGHT BEGINNINGS CHUMASH WORKBOOK will surely serve as a key component in assisting educators and parents to teach young children how to master language and grammar skills in a practical, enjoyable and educationally well-planned manner. It is evident that your talented staff invested a great deal of thought, time and effort into perfecting the method to give the gift of knowledge and skills to young children which they can utilize throughout their *chinuch* years, and beyond.

Much הצלחה to you and all of the staff at Yeshiva Darchei Noam for your continued success in educating our children בדרך ישראל סבא.

Sincerely,

Rabbi Dovid Nojowitz
Menahel
Torah Umesorah

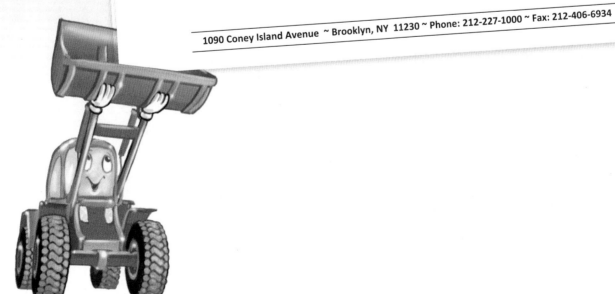

INTRODUCTION
to the Second Edition of Volume #1
BRIGHT BEGINNINGS
CHUMASH WORKBOOK

With much gratitude to Hashem, we are pleased to present the second edition of our Bright Beginnings Workbook on Parshas Lech Le'cha Volume One.

We are deeply gratified that the first edition of this workbook was warmly received by educators, students and parents worldwide. Along with the positive feedback, quite a number of people were kind enough to respond to our request for constructive criticism, and many of their suggestions have been incorporated in this second edition. With that in mind, we ask that you email your comments and suggestions to publications@thebrightbeginnings.com so we can make future editions even more user friendly.

By far the greatest "upgrade" to these pages is the *Hachana L'Chumash* section which pre-teaches the concepts of *sharashim, milim,* prefixes and suffixes, as well as introducing the 6 main prefixes. Acquiring these concepts prior to beginning Chumash study enables the children to recognize and translate a significant portion of the text immediately, which helps remove the paralyzing "fear factor" of encountering a foreign text. Furthermore, and perhaps more importantly, this empowers the teacher to focus on the comprehension of the text, as he/she will only need to review the technical language skills rather than introduce them for the very first time.

This workbook is designed for classroom use at the grade level when children are first introduced to Chumash. In addition to its use in a school setting, it can also be utilized at home should parents wish to enrich the Hebrew skills of their children. We have also found it to be an effective tool for adults who have a limited background in Judaic studies, and even for yeshiva graduates who were taught Chumash by rote in their childhood.

The workbook is intended to supplement the Chumash, not replace it. We recommend that children learn from a Chumash and use the workbook as a learning aid. Each *pasuk* (verse) is translated on a separate page and nearly all Hebrew words are translated on their own line. Be advised that due to the importance of maintaining the accuracy and consistency of each word's translation, the phrasing of an entire *pasuk* is occasionally clumsy. We began with *Parshas Lech Le'cha* instead of *Parshas Bereshis* because it contains root words found more commonly throughout Chumash, and the narrative is one that is simpler for the children to follow.

Please note that these workbooks are intended to provide a framework for educators and parents to introduce Chumash learning to children. We do not view this as a comprehensive educational script that includes all the review and drills needed to master *Lashon HaKodesh* at such a young age. Simply stated, these pages are just a beginning, not an end, and we encourage educators and parents to review and expand upon these lessons with the children long after they've "completed" these pages. Use the concepts of the exercises in these pages to review the lessons or draw on your own creativity to make other review tools for them.

The coloring and fonts of the words on the translation sheets are designed to draw the learner's attention to accurately match the root word and the prefix/suffix to its respective meaning. Some root words in each *pasuk* are pulled to the side and color-coded – green circles for nouns and blue squares for verbs – and each highlighted root word has a corresponding flash card located at the end of the booklet. Prefixes and suffixes and their translations are hollowed out as they are mastered, and there are flashcards to review the six most common prefixes encountered in Chumash. In this workbook series, we refer to the root word of a verb as a שרש and the root word of a noun as a מלה. Please note that many Jewish educators use the word שרש for the root word of both nouns and verbs, while others use terms such as שם עצם for nouns. The few adjectives introduced in this workbook are referred to as מלים as well, to simplify these concepts for the young children. With that in mind, our advice to parents is to use the same terms that your son's/daughter's teacher is using in school.

My dear friends Michael/Estelle Stein and Gershon/Aviva Distenfeld graciously underwrote the considerable expense of producing two informational audio-visual presentations which explain the educational philosophy that drives this workbook series. It can be viewed on the Bright Beginnings section of our website, https://thebrightbeginnings.com.

This workbook is dedicated in loving memory of Rabbi Meyer and Leya Zanitsky – HaRav Mordechai Meir ben Reb Yakov Eliyahu and Leah bas HaRav Yitzchak Mordechai *a"h* and we gratefully acknowledge the corporate sponsorship of these pages by Jerry and Barbara Weissman of Omni Managed Health. The *Hachana L'Chumash* section is dedicated to my childhood friend Marc Schertz *a"h* who tragically passed away at the age of 48. May his memory be for a blessing.

The content of these pages was lovingly created by Rabbi Yosef Binyomin Rawicki during the fifteen years that he served with distinction as first-grade Rebbi in Yeshiva Darchei Noam of Monsey. Mrs. Brocha Twersky spend an enormous amount of time since the first edition was released two years ago, upgrading the material included by creating the beautifully presented comprehensive new הכנה לחומש section found in the beginning of this workbook with the assistance of many talented Rebbeim and Moros around the country. On behalf of Jewish children worldwide and their teachers/parents who benefit from these pages, we thank them for their extraordinary dedication and passion to their holy work. We thank Mrs. Tova Leff for her stunning illustrations and beautiful cover and Mrs. Dena Peker and her incredibly talented staff at Dynagrafik Design Studios for their magnificent efforts in preparing the graphics to accompany the text. This workbook would never have reached the finish line without the active participation of the administrative director of The Center for Jewish Family Life/Project YES, Mrs. Chaya Becker, who served as this book's General Editor with boundless energy, devotion and commitment to excellence.

We are in the process of creating a series of educational workbooks on Chumash, Mishnah and Gemara in the Bright Beginnings Series that will develop a lifelong love for learning in our children and grandchildren by introducing them to learning in an enjoyable manner. Getting these materials from concept to final product requires a very significant investment, and I ask readers of these lines who have the capacity to contribute funds to Bright Beginnings or who would perhaps consider dedicating a volume to kindly contact me at publications@thebrightbeginnings. com or by calling 845-426-2243.

To our dear children; Baruch/Alanna Horowitz, Shlomie/Kaila Horowitz, Leah/ Moshe Webster, Faigy/Dovid Meir Loeb, and Sara; thank you for sharing me so graciously with the klal and for giving Mommy and me such unending *nachas*. Many times over the past thirty-four years, my wife, Udi, has offered her incredible range of talents to help me actualize my dreams. She is my partner in manning our Project YES helpline and is the go-to person for handling the sales and distribution of the Bright Beginnings Series. May Hashem repay her with our greatest wish – that we grow old together and share *nachas* from our wonderful children and grandchildren.

Finally, and most importantly, I would like to humbly give thanks to Hashem for allowing me to 'dwell in His House' *(Tehilim 27:4)* and to teach His Torah for the past thirty-three years.

May it be His will that these pages bring us closer to actualize our dream of *V'chol banayich limudei Hashem (Yeshayahu 54:13)* that each and every one of our children become proud, committed and learned Jews.

Yakov Horowitz
Monsey N.Y.

1 Elul 5774

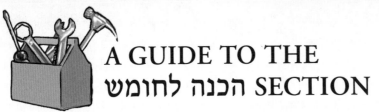

A GUIDE TO THE הכנה לחומש SECTION

THIS NEW SECTION OF THE WORKBOOK IS DIVIDED INTO TWO MAIN SEGMENTS, WITH MULTIPLE LESSONS AND REVIEW SHEETS CONTAINED HEREIN.

Segment #1: שרשים and מלים - The Concept of Root Words as Building Blocks

Lessons 1-4: These lessons introduce the concept of a שרש as the building block of many words that the student will encounter in the text. The opening lesson displays three different words that all contain the same שרש and is designed to teach the learner that all words containing these letters - and henceforth this שרש - are related. We began with the *shoresh* א-מ-ר so that the children can recognize their very first word in the פרשה!

The students are subsequently introduced to the concept of prefixes/suffixes. This will empower them to break down words into three segments: First by finding and identifying the שרש, and then by labeling all the letters found before the שרש as the prefix, and the letters following the שרש as the suffix. Learners are given the opportunity to review and internalize this method of breaking down words through various exercises.

Lessons 5-6: These lessons introduce the student to two new *Sharashim* ר-א-ה and ה-ל-כ. They are also introduced to a crucial rule, namely that the letters י-ו-נ-ה are frequently dropped from a שרש when it is "built" into a word. Although this may seem like a somewhat challenging idea for young children, it is a very relevant one - after all, פסוק א' alone contains **two** words demonstrating this concept - לך and וארא! The adorable יונה bird serves as a friendly mascot reminder of this rule!

Lessons 7-9: These lessons introduce the student to the concept of nouns (שם עצם) - referred to in this workbook as מלים - as another type of root word that can be found in the פסוקים. The student is introduced to four common nouns that are found almost immediately in Parshas Lech Lecha - בית, הר, אהל and ארץ.

Segment #2 - Identifying Prefixes and Suffixes

This segment in ***Lessons 10-16*** introduces the students to the six main prefixes: ה-ב-ל-מ-ו-כ. Each prefix lesson contains four review exercises. Additionally, there are cumulative review sheets added at appropriate intervals to provide the student with the opportunity for further comprehensive review. Flashcards are found at the end of the book for the student to use to review each of these prefixes.

We have inserted ***Lesson 17*** in פרק י"ב prior to learning פסוק ה', presenting the suffix ה. The letter ה after a מלה (specifically a place) means "to." This conjugation is found frequently in both פרק י"ב and פרק י"ג.

Later in the workbook, prior to beginning פרק י"ג, we inserted ***Lesson 18*** to introduce the children to the prefix א, which usually means "I will" and in certain circumstances can mean "I did" and ***Lesson 19*** to introduce the prefix י which usually means "He will" and in certain circumstances can mean "He did." The *Vov H'hepuch* is very briefly touched upon, and teachers may want to utilize this opportunity to focus on this concept at their discretion.

All of these new skills are built and expanded upon in Volume II of Bright Beginnings on Chumash Parshas Lech Le'cha, where the children are taught to recognize an additional 19 *Sharashim* and new configurations of prefixes and suffixes along with a cumulative review, utilizing the innovative and fun ***ShoreshLand*** game.

הֲכָנָה לְחוּמָשׁ

The הכנה לחומש section is dedicated
to my childhood friend **MARC SCHERTZ**
לזכר נשמת מנחם מנדל בן ר' משה ע"ה
who tragically passed away
8 Menachem Av 5774 at the age of 48.

*May the learning of thousands of Jewish children worldwide,
who benefit from these pages, be a Ze'chus for his Neshama.*

Rabbi Yakov Horowitz

מַזָּל טוֹב ON YOUR NEW חוּמָשׁ!

When you open up your new חוּמָשׁ
for the very first time, you will see many words.
All of these words will look different to you.

Actually, many of the words in the חוּמָשׁ are similar to each other.
This is because they share the same **root word or שֶׁרֶשׁ**.

What does this mean?

Let's learn our very first שֶׁרֶשׁ!

1. say   א-מ-ר

א-מ-ר is an example of a שֶׁרֶשׁ. This שֶׁרֶשׁ means "say".

There are many different words in the חוּמָשׁ that are built on the
שֶׁרֶשׁ of א-מ-ר. The translation of **all** of these words is similar.

> and he said - וַיֹּאמֶר
>
> I said - אָמַרְתִּי
>
> to say - לֵאמֹר

Color the letters א-מ-ר blue in the words below.
The first word has been completed for you.

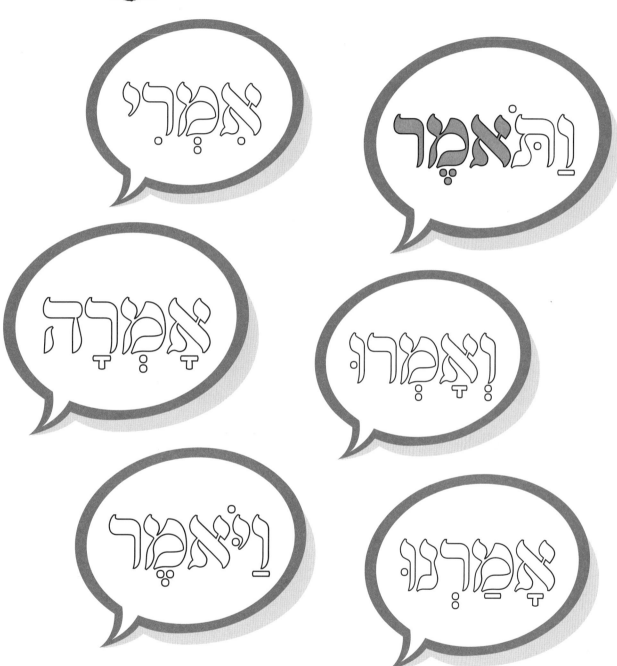

What is the meaning of the שֹׁרֶשׁ

א-מ-ר? _____

INTRODUCTION TO PREFIXES AND SUFFIXES

The letters that are found before and after the
שֹׁרֶשׁ in a word add meaning to the שֹׁרֶשׁ.

The letters that are found **before** the שֹׁרֶשׁ are called prefixes.

The letters that are found **after** the שֹׁרֶשׁ are called suffixes.

Suffix   שֹׁרֶשׁ   Prefix

Some words may only have a prefix:

שֹׁרֶשׁ   Prefix

Some words may only have a suffix:

Suffix   שֹׁרֶשׁ

INTRODUCTION TO PREFIXES AND SUFFIXES EXERCISE

1. Color the letters א-מ-ר blue in the words below.

2. Color the prefixes red. Some words may not have a prefix.

3. Color the suffixes yellow. Some words may not have a suffix.

The first word has been completed for you.

Remember:
A prefix is a letter **before** the שֹׁרֶשׁ.
A suffix is a letter **after** the שֹׁרֶשׁ.

The letters of a שֹׁרֶשׁ must always be
found in the same order:

1. Draw a ✔ in the box next to each word
   that has the שֹׁרֶשׁ א-מ-ר.

2. Draw an ✖ in the box next to each word
   that does not have the שֹׁרֶשׁ א-מ-ר.

□ אֲרמו

□ אמרו

□ תראמ

Now let's learn another שֹׁרֶשׁ!

2. bless   ב-ר-כ

1. Draw a line from the שֹׁרֶשׁ to its picture.

א-מ-ר

ב-ר-כ

2. Answer the question below.

What is the meaning of the שֹׁרֶשׁ ב-ר-כ? _____

LESSON 4

1. Color the letters ב-ר-כ blue in the pictures below.

2. Color the prefixes red. Some words may not have a prefix.

3. Color the suffixes yellow. Some words may not have a suffix.

The first word has been completed for you.

Remember:
A prefix is a letter **before** the שֹׁרֶשׁ.
A suffix is a letter **after** the שֹׁרֶשׁ.

REVIEW שָׁרָשִׁים א-מ-ר, ב-ר-כ

Look at the words on the bottom of the page.

1. Find the words with the שֹׁרֶשׁ א-מ-ר. Color the letters א-מ-ר blue. Color the prefixes red and the suffixes yellow.

2. Find the words with the שֹׁרֶשׁ ב-ר-כ. Color the letters ב-ר-כ blue. Color the prefixes red and the suffixes yellow.

3. Cut out all of the words.

4. Paste the words that have the שֹׁרֶשׁ א-מ-ר into the א-מ-ר column and the words that have the שֹׁרֶשׁ ב-ר-כ into the ב-ר-כ column.

שֹׁרֶשׁ ב-ר-כ	שֹׁרֶשׁ א-מ-ר

Remember: A prefix is a letter **before** the שֹׁרֶשׁ. A suffix is a letter **after** the שֹׁרֶשׁ.

וַאֲבָרְכָה מְבָרְכֶיךָ אָמַרְתִּי

וְאָמַרְתִּי נְבָרֵךְ וַיֹּאמֶר

Let's learn 2 new שָׁרָשִׁים!

3. go/went   ה-ל-כ

4. see   ר-א-ה

1. Draw a line from the שֹׁרֶשׁ to its picture.

2. Answer the questions below.

What is the meaning of the שֹׁרֶשׁ ה-ל-כ? _____

What is the meaning of the שֹׁרֶשׁ ר-א-ה? _____

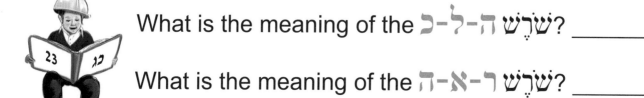

There are some שֹׁרֶשׁ letters that may "drop" from the שֹׁרֶשׁ.
When you look at a word in חוּמָשׁ, you will notice that one or
more of the שֹׁרֶשׁ letters is missing.

The letters that are most commonly
dropped from שָׁרָשִׁים are

י-ו-נ-ה.

hint! The letters ה-נ-ו-י fly away just like the יוֹנָה bird flies!

Examples:

שֹׁרֶשׁ ה-ל-כ
The letter ה was dropped in the words below

I will go - אֵלֵךְ

you will go - תֵּלְכִי

go - לֵךְ

שֹׁרֶשׁ ר-א-ה
The letter ה was dropped in the words below

I saw - רָאִיתִי

we saw - רָאִינוּ

they saw - רָאוּ

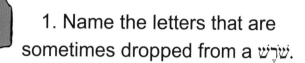

1. Name the letters that are sometimes dropped from a שֹׁרֶשׁ.

_____ _____ _____ _____

2. Color the letters ה-ל-כ blue in the words below.
Remember, the letter ה may be missing!

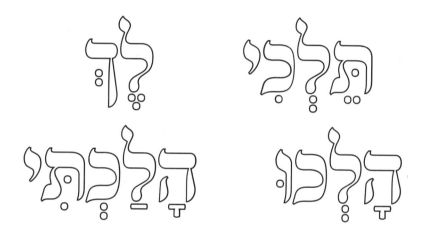

3. Color the letters ר-א-ה blue in the words below.
Remember, the letter ה may be missing!

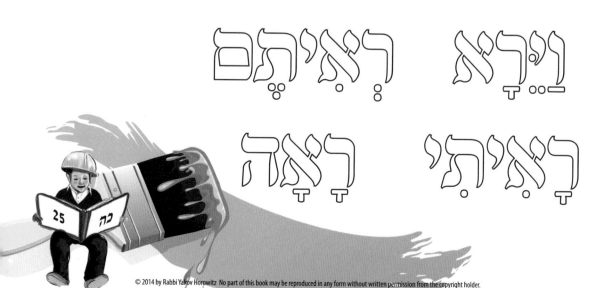

LESSON 6

DROPPED LETTERS י-ו-נ-ה EXERCISE

1. Color the letters כ-ל-ה blue in the words below. **Remember
that the letter ה may be missing.** Next, color the prefixes red.
Finally, color the suffixes yellow.

2. Color the letters ר-א-ה blue in the words below.
Remember that the letter ה may be missing. Next, color
the prefixes red. Finally, color the suffixes yellow.

Remember:
A prefix is a letter
before the שֹׁרֶשׁ.
A suffix is a letter
after the שֹׁרֶשׁ.

1. Draw a line from the שֹׁרֶשׁ to its meaning.

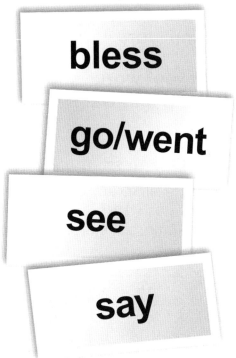

bless

go/went

see

say

א-מ-ר

ב-ר-כ

ה-ל-כ

ר-א-ה

2. Draw a line from the word to its שֹׁרֶשׁ.

א-מ-ר

ב-ר-כ

ה-ל-כ

ר-א-ה

מְבָרֶכְךָ

לֵךְ

וַיֹּאמֶר

רָאִיתִי

You may have noticed that every שֹׁרֶשׁ that you have learned is an
action word or verb - something that you **do**.
Examples: say, see, walk, bless.

A שֹׁרֶשׁ is always a verb **- or an action word.**

Now we are going to learn about another type of root word - the שֵׁם עֶצֶם
or noun. A שֵׁם עֶצֶם/ noun is a person, place, or thing and will be referred
to in this book as a מִלָּה.

Look around your classroom - you may see your סֵפֶר (book), your כִּסֵּא (chair) and the
דֶּלֶת (door.) You may also see another יֶלֶד (boy.) These are all examples of מִלִּים.

It is important to know that some words may have a מִלָּה as their root instead of a שֹׁרֶשׁ.

מִלִּים
סֵפֶר (book)
כִּסֵּא (chair)
יֶלֶד (boy)

שָׁרָשִׁים
ה-ל-כ (go/went)
א-מ-ר (say)
ב-ר-כ (bless)

Draw a picture of a "thing"
in your classroom.

מִלָּה

Draw a picture of yourself
doing an action.

שֹׁרֶשׁ

מִלָה: בַּיִת

 Let's learn our first מִלָה!

> On what street is your בַּיִת?

1. house בַּיִת

בַּיִת is an example of a מִלָה. This מִלָה means "house".

There are many different words in the חוּמָשׁ that are built on the מִלָה בַּיִת. The translation of **all** of these words is similar.

my house	בֵּיתִי
the house	הַבַּיִת
his house	בֵּיתוֹ

Color the letters of the מִלָה בַּיִת green in the words below. Next, color the prefixes red. Finally, color the suffixes yellow.
The first word has been completed for you.

כט 29

LESSON 9

Below are 3 new מִלִים

2. land — אֶרֶץ

3. tent — אֹהֶל

4. mountain — הַר

שׁ+מוֹה
Think of
הַר סִינַי!

Draw a picture of each מִלָה.

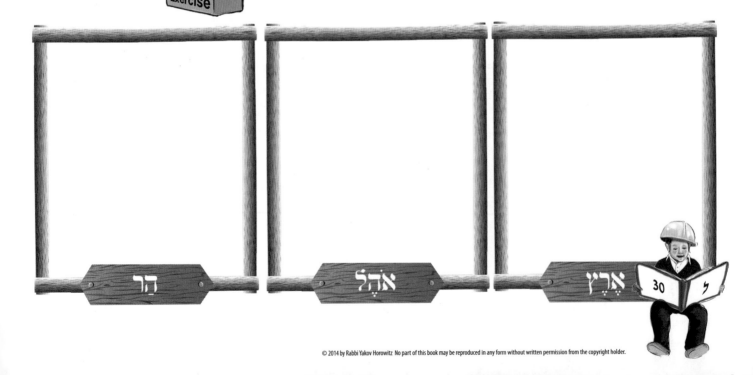

הַר · · · אֹהֶל · · · אֶרֶץ

EXERCISE מִלִּים אֶרֶץ, אֹהֶל, הַר

Color the letters of the מִלָּה אֶרֶץ green in the words below.
Color the prefixes red. Color the suffixes yellow.

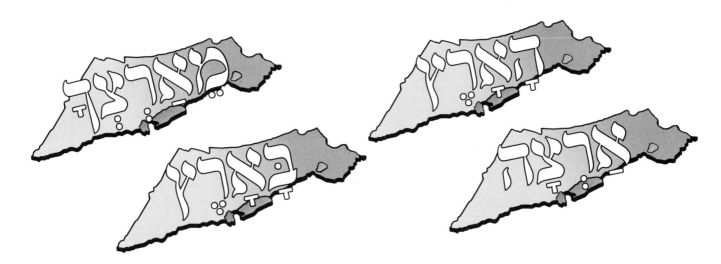

Color the letters of the מִלָּה הַר green in the words below.
Color the prefixes red.

Color the letters of the מִלָּה אֹהֶל green in the words below.
Color the prefixes red. Color the suffixes yellow.

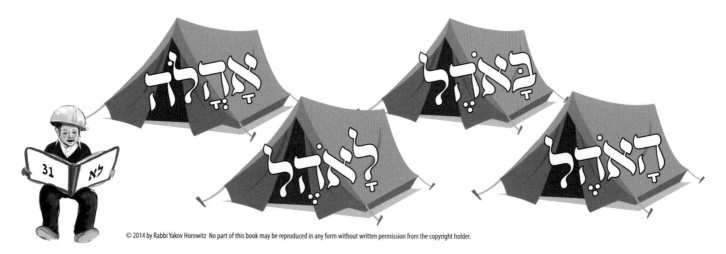

1. Draw a line from the מִלָּה to its meaning.

house

tent

mountain

land

אֹהֶל

הַר

בַּיִת

אֶרֶץ

2. Draw a line from the מִלָּה to the word that contains it.

מֵאַרְצְךָ

הָהָר

בָּאֹהֶל

בְּבֵיתֶךָ

אֹהֶל

הַר

בַּיִת

אֶרֶץ

As you have learned, the prefixes and suffixes that are found **BEFORE** and **AFTER** שָׁרָשִׁים and מִלִּים add meaning to the שֹׁרֶשׁ or מִלָּה.

As you learn חוּמָשׁ, you will learn the meaning of each of the prefixes and suffixes. This will enable you to understand the complete meaning of almost every word that you see! Below are the **6 main prefixes** that you will learn as part of the introduction to פָּרָשַׁת לֶךְ לְךָ.

the	-	הַ
in / with	-	בְּ
from	-	מִ
to / for	-	לְ
and	-	וְ
like	-	כְּ

33 לג

rule:

Whenever there is a ה prefix before a מִלָה it means **the**.

Examples of the ה prefix:

the land - הָאָרֶץ

the house - הַבַּיִת

the tent - הָאֹהֶל

the mountain - הָהָר

Now it's your turn!
Add the prefix ה to the מִלָּה.

1. the house - ____בַּיִת

2. the tent - ____אֹהֶל

3. the land - ____אֶרֶץ

4. the mountain - ____הַר

Can you draw a picture of הַבַּיִת?

Can you draw a picture of הָאֹהֶל?

It's time for art!

LESSON 11

 Draw a line from the word to the correct meaning.

3
the house
house
בַּיִת

1
the land
land
הָאָרֶץ

4
the land
land
אֶרֶץ

2
the tent
tent
הָאֹהֶל

Write the number of the correct word on the line.

_____the house   אֶרֶץ .1

_____the land   הַבַּיִת .2

_____land   הָאֹהֶל .3

_____the tent   הָאָרֶץ .4

_____house   בַּיִת .5

_____tent   אֹהֶל .6

36

rule:

Whenever there is a בּ prefix before a מִלָּה it means **in** or **with**.

 Generally, if the נְקוּדָה under the בּ is a פַּתַח, סֶגּוֹל, or קָמֵץ (בָּ, בֶּ, בַ), the בּ will be translated as **in the**.

Examples of the בּ prefix:

in יְרוּשָׁלַיִם - בִּירוּשָׁלַיִם

in אֶרֶץ יִשְׂרָאֵל - בְּאֶרֶץ יִשְׂרָאֵל

in the house - בַּבַּיִת

in the tent - בָּאֹהֶל

PREFIX בּ EXERCISE

Now it's your turn!
Add the prefix בּ to the מִלָּה.

.1 in יְרוּשָׁלַיִם - יְרוּשָׁלַיִם _____

.2 in אֶרֶץ יִשְׂרָאֵל - אֶרֶץ יִשְׂרָאֵל _____

.3 in the house - בַּיִת _____

.4 in the tent - אֹהֶל _____

Draw a line from the word to the correct meaning.

3

land
the land
in the land

אֶרֶץ

1

house
the house
in the house

בַּבַּיִת

4

mountain
the mountain
in the mountain

הָהָר

2

tent
the tent
in the tent

בָּאֹהֶל

Write the number of the correct word on the line.

_____house   בָּאָרֶץ .1

_____in the land   אֶרֶץ .2

_____in the tent   בַּבַּיִת .3

_____tent   בַּיִת .4

_____land   בָּאֹהֶל .5

_____in the house   אֹהֶל .6

PREFIXES ה AND ב REVIEW

Cut out the word boxes at the bottom of the page.
Paste each word box to its meaning to create a picture!

house	the house	in the house
tent	the tent	in the tent
mountain	the mountain	in the mountain
land	the land	in the land

41

מא

INTRODUCING

Prefix #3

from - מ

rule:

Whenever there is a מ prefix before a מִלָּה it means **from**.

Examples of the מ prefix:

from יְרוּשָׁלַיִם - מִירוּשָׁלַיִם

from מִצְרַיִם - מִמִּצְרַיִם

In the examples below, there is more
than one prefix before the מִלָּה.

from the house - מֵהַבַּיִת

from the tent - מֵהָאֹהֶל

LESSON 13

Now it's your turn!
Add the prefix מ to the מִלָה.

from יְרוּשָׁלַיִם - יְרוּשָׁלַיִם _____

Now it's your turn!
Add the prefix מ and ה to the מִלָה below.

from the house - בַּיִת _____

Where is he from?

1. Match the person to the place they are from:

מִצְרַיִם

שׁוֹשַׁן הַבִּירָה

אֶסְתֵּר הַמַּלְכָּה

פַּרְעֹה

מָרְדְּכַי הַצַּדִּיק

2. Where are **YOU** from? _____ מ

44 דף

© 2014 by Rabbi Yakov Horowitz No part of this book may be reproduced in any form without written permission from the copyright holder.

PREFIX מ EXERCISE

Draw a line from the word to the correct meaning.

3
tent
the tent
from the tent
מֵהָאֹהֶל

1
house
the house
from the house
מֵהַבַּיִת

4
land
the land
from the land
הָאָרֶץ

2
mountain
the mountain
from the mountain
הַר

Write the number of the correct word on the line.

_____from the land   מִירוּשָׁלַיִם .1

_____house   מֵהָאָרֶץ .2

_____from the tent   מֵהַבַּיִת .3

_____from יְרוּשָׁלַיִם   מֵאֶרֶץ יִשְׂרָאֵל .4

_____from the house   מֵהָאֹהֶל .5

_____from אֶרֶץ יִשְׂרָאֵל   בַּיִת .6

מה 45

rule:

Whenever there is a ל prefix before a מִלָּה or שֹׁרֶשׁ it means **to** or **for**.

Generally, if the נְקוּדָה under the ל is a קָמַץ or סֶגּוֹל, פַּתַח (לָ, לֶ, לְ), the ל will be translated as **to the**.

In the examples below, the ל prefix is found before מִלִּים:

to יְרוּשָׁלַיִם - לִירוּשָׁלַיִם

to אֶרֶץ יִשְׂרָאֵל - לְאֶרֶץ יִשְׂרָאֵל

to the house - לְבַיִת

to the tent - לְאֹהֶל

In the example below, the ל prefix is found before a שֹׁרֶשׁ:

to bless - לְבָרֵךְ

Prefix ל Exercise

Now it's your turn!
Add the prefix ל to the מִלָה or שֹׁרֶשׁ.

1. to the house - בַּיִת____

2. to the tent - אֹהֶל____

3. to יְרוּשָׁלַיִם - יְרוּשָׁלַיִם____

4. to bless - בָּרֵךְ____

Look at the pictures, then add the correct prefix to answer the questions.

Where is the boy going?

He is going

בַּיִת____.

Where is the boy going?

He is going

אֹהֶל____.

PREFIX לְ EXERCISE

 Draw a line from the word to the correct meaning.

3

the land
land
to the land

אֶרֶץ

1

house
the house
to the house

לַבַּיִת

4

tent
the tent
to the tent

לְאֹהֶל

2

mountain
the mountain
to the mountain

הַר

 Write the number of the correct word on the line.

_____to bless

לָאָרֶץ .1

_____to the tent

לַבַּיִת .2

_____to the land

לִירוּשָׁלַיִם .3

_____to יְרוּשָׁלַיִם

לְבָרֵךְ .4

_____land

לְאֹהֶל .5

_____to the house

אֶרֶץ .6

Exercise

Color each prefix the same color as its meaning.

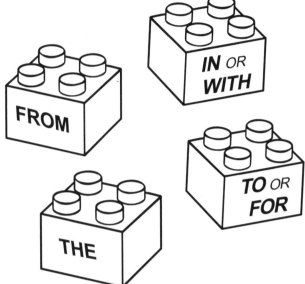

FROM

IN OR WITH

THE

TO OR FOR

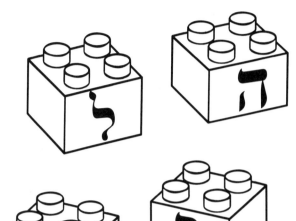

ל

ה

מ

ב

 **Exercise**

Look at the pictures. Then, add the prefix ל, ב or מ to answer the question.

Where is the boy?

The boy is

בַּיִת___.

Where is the boy coming from?

He is coming

אֹהֶל___.

Where is the boy going?

He is going

יְרוּשָׁלַיִם___.

מט 49

PREFIXES מ AND ל, ב, ה REVIEW

1. Choose a color for each מִלָּה on the left side of the page.

2. Color the מִלָּה.

3. Color each word on the right side of the page using the same color as its מִלָּה.

PREFIXES מ AND ל, ב, ה REVIEW

Exercise

Cut out the word boxes at the bottom of the page.
Paste each word box to its meaning to create a picture!

in the tent	from the tent	to the tent
in the house	from the house	to the house
in the mountain	from the mountain	to the mountain
in the land	from the land	to the land

מֵהָאָרֶץ   לַבַּיִת   מֵהַבַּיִת

לָהַר   מֵהָאֹהֶל   מֵהַהַר

בָּאֹהֶל   בָּהַר   *learning prefixes!* בַּבַּיִת
I'm having a ball

בָּאָרֶץ   לָאֹהֶל   לָאָרֶץ

51

rule:

Whenever there is a וֹ prefix before a מִלָה or שֹׁרֶשׁ it means **and**.

Examples of the וֹ prefix:

land and house - אֶרֶץ וּבַיִת

tent and land - אֹהֶל וָאֶרֶץ

house and tent - בַּיִת וָאֹהֶל

You will notice that there is a prefix in the words below that you have not yet learned. This letter is black. You will learn its meaning at a later time.

and he blessed - וַיְבָרֶךְ

and he said - וַיֹּאמֶר

Extra Credit! Can you guess what the prefix ' means? ___

Now it's your turn!
Add the prefix ו to the שֹׁרֶשׁ or מִלָּה.

house and tent - בַּיִת ____אֹהֶל .1

tent and land - אֹהֶל ____אֶרֶץ .2

and he blessed - יְבָרֵךְ____ .3

and he said - יֹאמֶר____ .4

Add the correct prefix to describe the pictures.

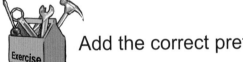

בַּיִת __אֹהֶל

הַר __אֹהֶל

הַר __בַּיִת

LESSON 15

 Draw a line from the word to the correct meaning.

3 tent / and tent / from the tent — וְאֹהֶל	**1** land / from the land / and land — וְאֶרֶץ
4 house / from the house / and house — וּבַיִת	**2** mountain / from the mountain / and the mountain — הַר

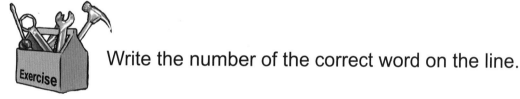 Write the number of the correct word on the line.

_____house and mountain .1 אֶרֶץ וְאֹהֶל

_____land and house .2 וַיְבָרֶךְ

_____and he said .3 וַיֹּאמֶר

_____and he blessed .4 אֶרֶץ וּבַיִת

_____land and tent .5 בַּיִת וְהַר

55 נה

© 2014 by Rabbi Yakov Horowitz No part of this book may be reproduced in any form without written permission from the copyright holder.

INTRODUCING

Prefix #6

like - כ

rule:

Whenever there is a כ prefix before a מִלָה it means **like**.

Did you know?

Generally, if the נְקוּדָה under the כ is a קָמַץ, סֶגּוֹל, פַּתַח, or (כָ, כֶ, כַ), the כ will be translated as **like the**.

Examples of the כ prefix:

like יְרוּשָׁלַיִם - כִּירוּשָׁלַיִם

like מֹשֶׁה - כְּמֹשֶׁה

like the house - כַּבַּיִת

like the tent - כָּאֹהֶל

like the land - כָּאָרֶץ

like the mountain - כָּהָר

56

PREFIX כ EXERCISE

Now it's your turn!
Add the prefix כ to the מִלָּה.

.1 like יְרוּשָׁלַיִם - יְרוּשָׁלַיִם _____

.2 like מֹשֶׁה - מֹשֶׁה _____

.3 בַּיִת _____ - like the house

.4 אֹהֶל _____ - like the tent

1. Who do you want to be like when you grow up? Your סַבָּא? Your רֶבִּי? Your אַבָּא?

When I grow up I want to be

כְּ_____ !

2. Boys are bentched that they should be like אֶפְרַיִם and מְנַשֶׁה. This בְּרָכָה is below. Fill in the missing prefixes to complete the בְּרָכָה:

May ה' establish you - יְשִׂמְךָ אֱלֹקִים

_____ אֶפְרַיִם - אֶפְרַיִם like

וְ_____ מְנַשֶׁה - מְנַשֶׁה and like

Draw a line from the word to the correct meaning.

3

like the tent
from the tent
to the tent

כָּאֹהֶל

1

like יְרוּשָׁלַיִם
to יְרוּשָׁלַיִם
from יְרוּשָׁלַיִם

כִּירוּשָׁלַיִם

4

like the house
in the house
to the house

בַּבַּיִת

2

in the mountain
like the mountain
from the mountain

כָּהָר

Write the number of the correct word on the line.

_____like the house   בַּבַּיִת .1

_____house   בַּיִת .2

_____like the tent   כִּירוּשָׁלַיִם .3

_____like יְרוּשָׁלַיִם   כָּאֹהֶל .4

_____like מֹשֶׁה   כְּמֹשֶׁה .5

_____tent   אֹהֶל .6

נח 58

Color each prefix the same color as its meaning.

FROM

LIKE

TO OR FOR

THE

IN OR WITH

AND

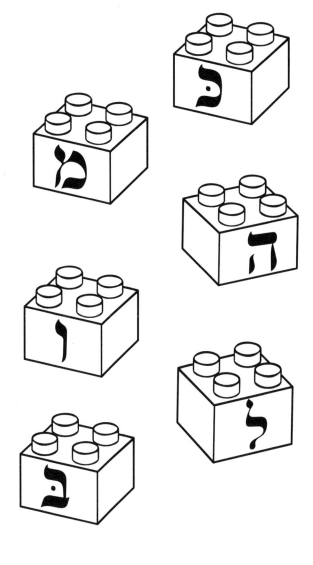

כ

מ

ה

ו

ל

ב

59

CUMULATIVE REVIEW

1. Write the meaning of each שֹׁרֶשׁ or מִלָּה on the line next to it.

2. Color the letters of the שֹׁרֶשׁ or מִלָּה in each word **black**.

3. Color each enlarged prefix (that you have already learned) according to the color chart below. The first example has been completed for you.

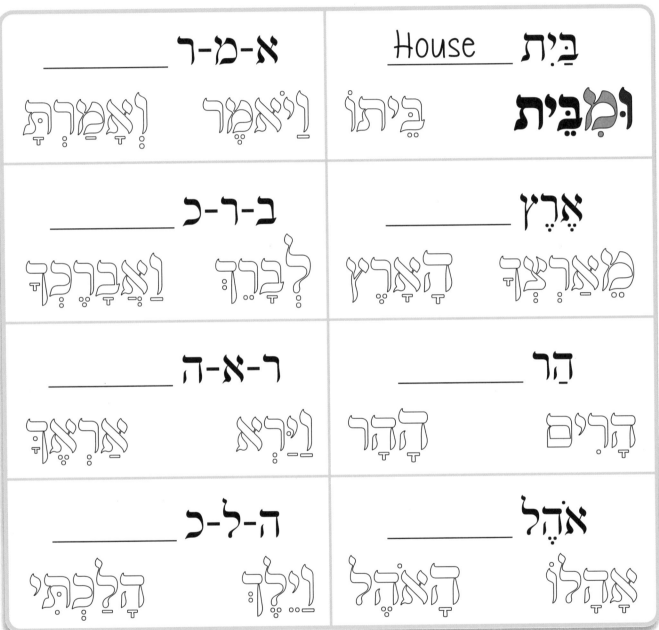

א-מ-ר _____	House בַּיִת
וְאָמַרְתָּ וַיֹּאמֶר	בֵּיתוֹ וּמִבֵּית
ב-ר-כ _____	אֶרֶץ _____
וַאֲבָרֶכְךָ לְבָרֵךְ	מֵאֶרֶץ הָאָרֶץ
ר-א-ה _____	הַר _____
אֵרֶא וַיַּרְא	הָהָר הָרִים
ה-ל-כ _____	אֹהֶל _____
הָלַכְתִּי וַיֵּלֶךְ	הָאֹהֶל אֹהֱלוֹ

COLOR CHART

AND = PURPLE
THE = GREEN
FROM = BLUE
IN/WITH = RED
TO/FOR = PINK
LIKE = ORANGE

פָּרָשַׁת

לֶךְ לְךָ

פֶּרֶק יב

Color each שֹׁרֶשׁ or מִלָּה the same color as its meaning.
Some meanings will not be used.

HOUSE

SAY

SEE / APPEAR /
SHOW / LOOK /
VISION

LAND

GO / WENT

BLESS

אמר

הלך

בַּיִת

אֶרֶץ

רָאה

English	Hebrew	Root
And **He** said	וַיֹּאמֶר	**אמר**
ה' הַשֵּׁם	ה'	
to **אַבְרָם** to	אֶל אַבְרָם	
go	לֶךְ	**הלכ**
for **you**	לְךָ	
from **your** land	מֵאַרְצְךָ	**אֶרֶץ**
and from **your birth place**	וּמִמּוֹלַדְתְּךָ	
and from **the** house of	וּמִבֵּית	**בֵּית**
your father	אָבִיךָ	
to the land	אֶל הָאָרֶץ	**אֶרֶץ**
that	אֲשֶׁר	
I will **show** you	אַרְאֶךָּ:	**ראה**

Color each prefix using the color chart below.

וַיֹּאמֶר לְךָ

מֵאַרְצְךָ

וּמִמּוֹלַדְתְּךָ

וּמִבֵּית הָאָרֶץ

COLOR CHART

AND = BLUE

THE = RED

FROM = GREEN

IN / WITH = ORANGE

TO / FOR = PINK

LIKE = PURPLE

1. Choose a color for each מִלָה or שֹׁרֶשׁ on the left side of the page.

2. Color the שֹׁרֶשׁ or מִלָה.

3. Color each word on the right side of the page using the same color as its מִלָה or שֹׁרֶשׁ.

Color each שֹׁרֶשׁ or מִלָּה the same color as its meaning.
Some meanings will not be used.

NAME

CALL

BLESS

DO / MAKE

שֵׁם

עשה

ברכ

English	Hebrew	Root
And **I will** make **you**	וְאֶעֶשְׂךָ	עשה
to **a nation**	לְגוֹי	
great	גָּדוֹל	
and **I will** bless **you**	וַאֲבָרֶכְךָ	ברכ
and **I will make great**	וַאֲגַדְּלָה	
your name	שְׁמֶךָ	שֵׁם
and **you will be**	וֶהְיֵה	
a blesser	בְּרָכָה:	ברכ

Color each prefix using the color chart below.

וְאֶעֶשְׂךָ לְגוֹי

וַאֲבָרֶכְךָ

וַאֲגַדְּלָה

וֶהְיֵה

COLOR CHART

AND = BLUE
THE = RED
FROM = GREEN
IN / WITH = ORANGE
TO / FOR = PINK
LIKE = PURPLE

סח 68

1. Choose a color for each מִלָּה or שֹׁרֶשׁ on the left side of the page.

2. Color the שֹׁרֶשׁ or מִלָּה.

3. Color each word on the right side of the page using the same color as its מִלָּה or שֹׁרֶשׁ.

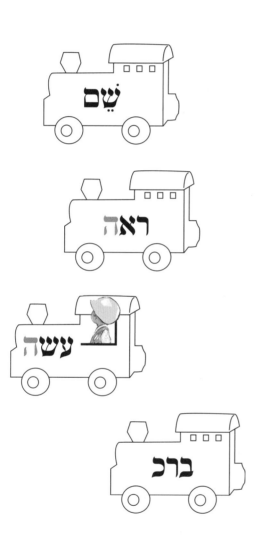

Color each שֹׁרֶשׁ or מִלָּה the same color as its meaning.
Some meanings will not be used.

HOUSE

FAMILY

BLESS

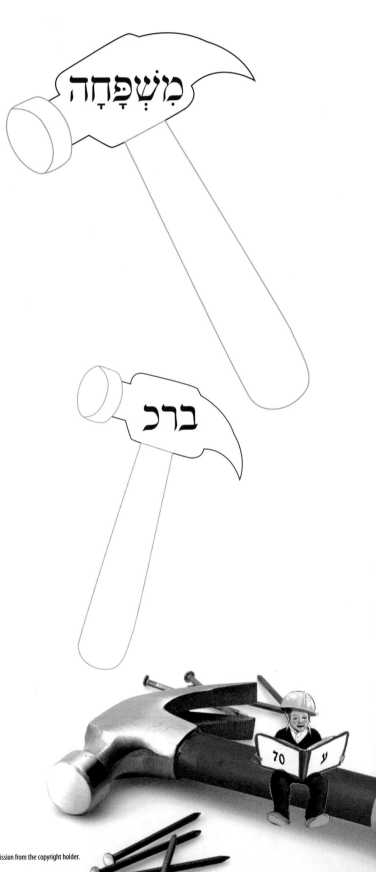

מִשְׁפָּחָה

ברכ

And I will bless	וַאֲבָרְכָה	בּרכ
those who bless you	מְבָרְכֶיךָ	בּרכ
and those who curse you	וּמְקַלֶּלְךָ	
I will curse	אָאֹר	
and they will be blessed	וְנִבְרְכוּ	בּרכ
with you	בְךָ	
all	כֹּל	
families of	מִשְׁפְּחֹת	מִשְׁפָּחָה
the earth	הָאֲדָמָה:	

Color each prefix using the color chart below.

וַאֲבָרְכָה

וּמְקַלֶּלְךָ

וְנִבְרְכוּ בְךָ

הָאֲדָמָה

COLOR CHART
AND = BLUE
THE = RED
FROM = GREEN
IN / WITH = ORANGE
TO / FOR = PINK
LIKE = PURPLE

1. Choose a color for each מִלָּה or שֹׁרֶשׁ on the left side of the page.

2. Color the שֹׁרֶשׁ or מִלָּה.

3. Color each word on the right side of the page using the same color as its שֹׁרֶשׁ or מִלָּה.

Color each שֹׁרֶשׁ or מִלָה the same color as its meaning.
Some meanings will not be used.

GO / WENT

GO OUT

YEAR

BLESS

שָׁנָה

הלכ

יצא

And he went	וַיֵּלֶךְ	הלך
אַבְרָם	אַבְרָם	
as	כַּאֲשֶׁר	
spoke	דִּבֶּר	
to him	אֵלָיו	
הַשֵׁם	ה'	
and he went	וַיֵּלֶךְ	הלך
with him	אִתּוֹ	
לוֹט	לוֹט	
and אַבְרָם was	וְאַבְרָם	
age of	בֶּן	
five years	חָמֵשׁ שָׁנִים	שָׁנָה
and seventy years	וְשִׁבְעִים שָׁנָה	שָׁנָה
when he went out	בְּצֵאתוֹ	יצא
from חָרָן	מֵחָרָן:	

עה 75

Color each prefix using the color chart below.

וַיֵּלֶךְ וְאַבְרָם
וְשִׁבְעִים
מֵחָרָן

COLOR CHART

AND = BLUE
THE = RED
FROM = GREEN
IN / WITH = ORANGE
TO / FOR = PINK
LIKE = PURPLE

פָּסוּק ד

1. Choose a color for each מִלָּה or שֹׁרֶשׁ on the left side of the page.

2. Color the מִלָּה or שֹׁרֶשׁ.

3. Color each word on the right side of the page using the same color as its שֹׁרֶשׁ or מִלָּה.

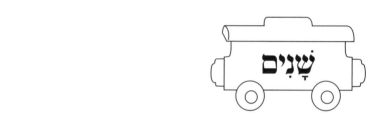

rule:

Whenever there is a ה after a place it means **to** that place.

Examples of the ה suffix:

Whenever there is a ה after a direction מִלָּה (North, South, East, West) it means **to** that direction.

to the land of כְּנַעַן - אַרְצָה כְּנַעַן

to מִצְרַיִם to - מִצְרַיְמָה

to the North - צָפֹנָה

to the South - נֶגְבָּה

to the East - קֵדְמָה

to the West - יָמָּה

צָפוֹן
NORTH

יָם
WEST

קֶדֶם
EAST

נֶגֶב
SOUTH

עח 78

Now it's your turn!
Add the suffix ה to the מִלָּה.

1. אַרְצָ___ כְּנַעַן - כְּנַעַן to the land of

2. מִצְרַיְמָ___ - מִצְרַיִם to

3. ___נֶגְבְּ - to the South

4. ___קֵדְמָ - to the East

Circle the prefix that has the same translation as the ה suffix:

עט 79

Lesson 17

1. Circle the picture of the boy who is going אַרְצָה כְּנַעַן:

2. Draw a picture of a boy going הַבַּיְתָה:

Lesson 17

 Draw a line from the word to the correct meaning.

3

to the East
from the East
East

קֵדְמָה

1

in אֶרֶץ כְּנַעַן
like אֶרֶץ כְּנַעַן
to אֶרֶץ כְּנַעַן

אַרְצָה כְּנַעַן

4

to the West
from the West
West

יָמָּה

2

like the house
in the house
to the house

הַבַּיְתָה

 Write the number of the correct word on the line.

_____to the house   צָפֹנָה .1

_____to the East   קֵדְמָה .2

_____in the house   הַבַּיְתָה .3

_____to the North   נֶגְבָּה .4

_____to the South   יָמָּה .5

_____to the West   בַּבַּיִת .6

81
אפ

Color each שֹׁרֶשׁ or מִלָה the same color as its meaning.
Some meanings will not be used.

FATHER

COME

WOMAN / WIFE

TAKE

GO / WENT

GO OUT

DO / MAKE

BROTHER

SOUL

לקח

אָח

הלך

אִשָּׁה

נֶפֶשׁ

בוא

עשה

יצא

And he took	וַיִּקַּח	לקח
Avram	אַבְרָם	
את שָׂרַי	אֶת שָׂרַי	
his wife	אִשְׁתּוֹ	אשה
and	וְאֶת לוֹט	
the son of his brother	בֶּן אָחִיו	אח
and all	וְאֶת כָּל	
their possessions	רְכוּשָׁם	
that they possessed	אֲשֶׁר רָכָשׁוּ	
and the souls (people)	וְאֶת הַנֶּפֶשׁ	נפש
that they made (believe in הַשֵּׁם)	אֲשֶׁר עָשׂוּ	עשה
in	בְּחָרָן	
and they went out	וַיֵּצְאוּ	יצא
to go	לָלֶכֶת	הלך
to the land of	אַרְצָה כְּנַעַן	ארץ
and they came	וַיָּבֹאוּ	בוא
to the land of	אַרְצָה כְּנָעַן:	ארץ

Color each prefix using the color chart below.

וַיִּקַּח וְאֶת

הַנֶּפֶשׁ וַיֵּצְאוּ

לָלֶכֶת

וַיָּבֹאוּ בְּחָרָן

COLOR CHART

AND = BLUE
THE = RED
FROM = GREEN
IN / WITH = ORANGE
TO / FOR = PINK
LIKE = PURPLE

פָּסוּק ה

1. Choose a color for each מִלָּה or שֹׁרֶשׁ on the left side of the page.

2. Color the שֹׁרֶשׁ or מִלָּה.

3. Color each word on the right side of the page using the same color as its שֹׁרֶשׁ or מִלָּה.

 Color each שֹׁרֶשׁ or מִלָּה the same color as its meaning.
Some meanings will not be used.

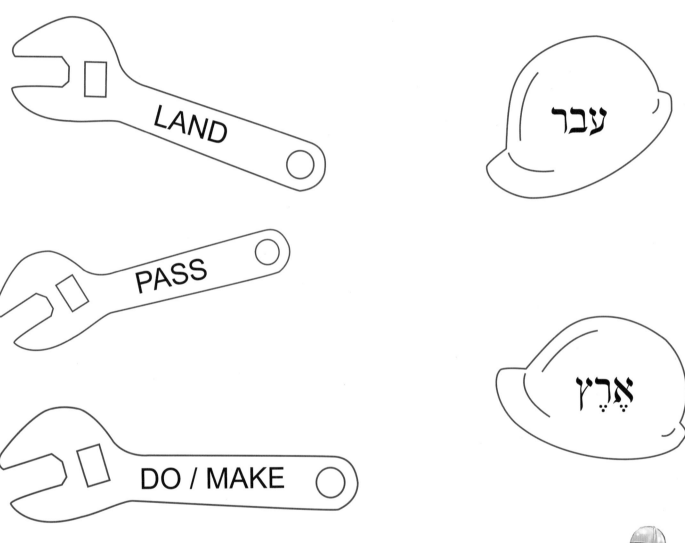

LAND

עבר

PASS

אֶרֶץ

DO / MAKE

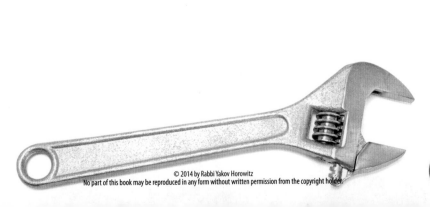

86 פו

And **he** passed through	וַיַּעֲבֹר	עבר
אַבְרָם	אַבְרָם	
in the land	בְּאֶרֶץ	אֶרֶץ
until	עַד	
the place of	מְקוֹם	
שְׁכֶם	שְׁכֶם	
until	עַד	
the plain of מוֹרֶה	אֵלוֹן מוֹרֶה	
and the כְּנַעֲנִי	וְהַכְּנַעֲנִי	
(were) then	אָז	
in the land	בָּאָרֶץ:	אֶרֶץ

Color each prefix using the color chart below.

וַיַּעֲבֹר

בְּאֶרֶץ

וְהַכְּנַעֲנִי

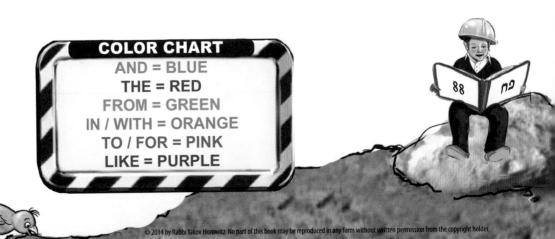

COLOR CHART
AND = BLUE
THE = RED
FROM = GREEN
IN / WITH = ORANGE
TO / FOR = PINK
LIKE = PURPLE

1. Choose a color for each מִלָּה or שֹׁרֶשׁ on the left side of the page.

2. Color the שֹׁרֶשׁ or מִלָּה.

3. Color each word on the right side of the page using the same color as its שֹׁרֶשׁ or מִלָּה.

Color each שֹׁרֶשׁ or מִלָּה the same color as its meaning.
Some meanings will not be used.

CHILDREN

HOUSE

GIVE

SAY

SEE / APPEAR /
SHOW / LOOK /
VISION

רָאָה

אָמַר

זֶרַע

נָתַן

90

And He appeared	וַיֵּרָא	רֹאה
הַשֵּׁם	ה'	
to אַבְרָם to	אֶל אַבְרָם	
and He said	וַיֹּאמֶר	אמר
to your children	לְזַרְעֲךָ	זֶרַע
I will give	אֶתֵּן	נתן
this land	אֶת הָאָרֶץ הַזֹּאת	אֶרֶץ
and he built	וַיִּבֶן	
there	שָׁם	
a מִזְבֵּחַ	מִזְבֵּחַ	
to הַשֵּׁם	לַה'	
that appeared	הַנִּרְאֶה	רֹאה
to him	אֵלָיו:	

Color each prefix using the color chart below.

וַיֵּרָא וַיֹּאמֶר

לְזַרְעֲךָ וַיִּבֶן

לַה׳

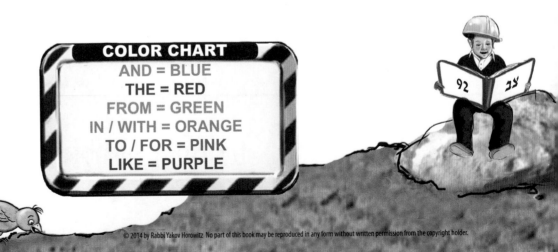

COLOR CHART

AND = BLUE
THE = RED
FROM = GREEN
IN / WITH = ORANGE
TO / FOR = PINK
LIKE = PURPLE

92   צב

1. Choose a color for each מִלָּה or שֹׁרֶשׁ on the left side of the page.

2. Color the שֹׁרֶשׁ or מִלָּה.

3. Color each word on the right side of the page using the same color as its מִלָּה or שֹׁרֶשׁ.

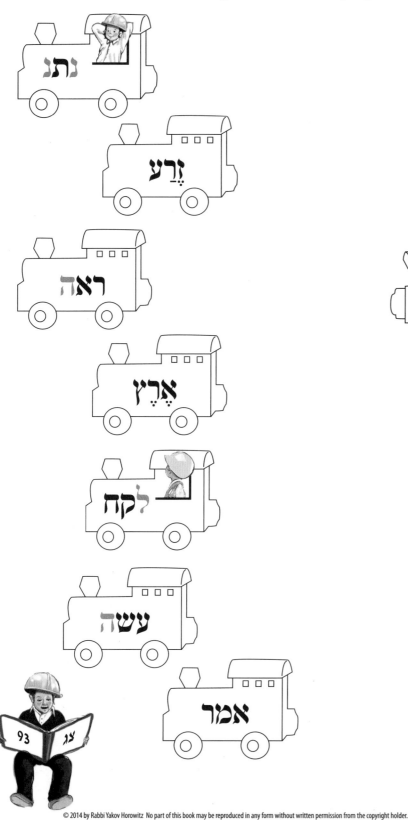

Color each שֹׁרֶשׁ or מִלָּה the same color as its meaning.
Some meanings will not be used.

EAST

NAME

TENT

SPEAK

CALL

MOUNTAIN

אֹהֶל

קרא

הַר

שֵׁם

קֶדֶם

And he moved	וַיַּעְתֵּק	
from there	מִשָּׁם	
to the mountain	הָהָרָה	הַר
from the east	מִקֶּדֶם	
to (the city)	לְבֵית אֵל בֵּית אֵל	
and he pitched	וַיֵּט	
his tent	אָהֳלֹה	אֹהֶל
	בֵּית אֵל בֵּית אֵל	
from the west	מִיָּם	
and the (city) עַי	וְהָעַי	
from the east	מִקֶּדֶם	
and he built	וַיִּבֶן	
there	שָׁם	
a מִזְבֵּחַ	מִזְבֵּחַ	
to הַשֵּׁם	לַה׳	
and he called	וַיִּקְרָא	קרא
in the name of הַשֵּׁם	בְּשֵׁם ה׳	שֵׁם

Color each prefix using the color chart below.

וַיַּעְתֵּק הָהָרָה

מִקֶּדֶם לְבֵית וַיֵּט

מַיְם וְהָעַי מִקֶּדֶם

וַיִּבֶן לַה' וַיִּקְרָא

בְּשֵׁם

COLOR CHART

AND = BLUE
THE = RED
FROM = GREEN
IN / WITH = ORANGE
TO / FOR = PINK
LIKE = PURPLE

96 צו

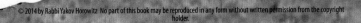

פָּסוּק ח

1. Choose a color for each מִלָּה or שֹׁרֶשׁ on the left side of the page.

2. Color the שֹׁרֶשׁ or מִלָּה.

3. Color each word on the right side of the page using the same color as its שֹׁרֶשׁ or מִלָּה.

Color each שֹׁרֶשׁ or מִלָּה the same color as its meaning.
Some meanings will not be used.

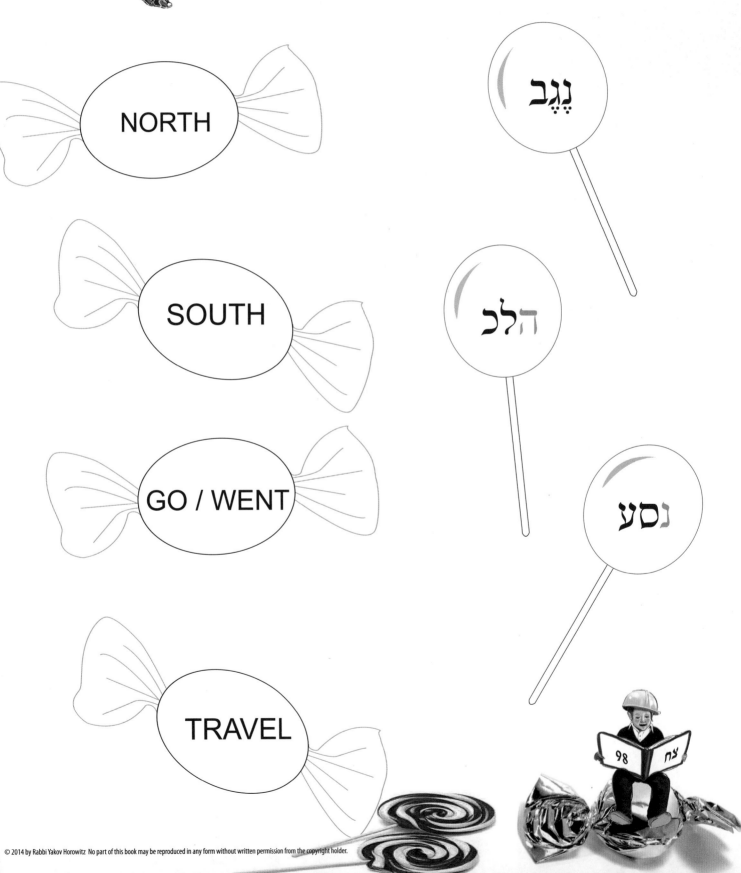

NORTH

נֶגֶב

SOUTH

הלך

GO / WENT

נסע

TRAVEL

98

And **he travel**ed	וַיִּסַּע	**נסע**
אַבְרָם	אַבְרָם	
going	הָלוֹךְ	**הלכ**
and **travel**ing	וְנָסוֹעַ	**נסע**
to the **south side**	הַנֶּגְבָּה:	

Color each prefix using the color chart below.

וַיִּסַּע

וְנָסוֹעַ

הַנֶּגְבָּה

COLOR CHART

AND = BLUE
THE = RED
FROM = GREEN
IN / WITH = ORANGE
TO / FOR = PINK
LIKE = PURPLE

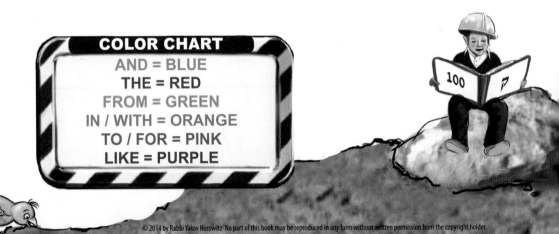

1. Choose a color for each מִלָּה or שֹׁרֶשׁ on the left side of the page.

2. Color the שֹׁרֶשׁ or מִלָּה.

3. Color each word on the right side of the page using the same color as its מִלָּה or שֹׁרֶשׁ.

Color each שֹׁרֶשׁ or מִלָּה the same color as its meaning.
Some meanings will not be used.

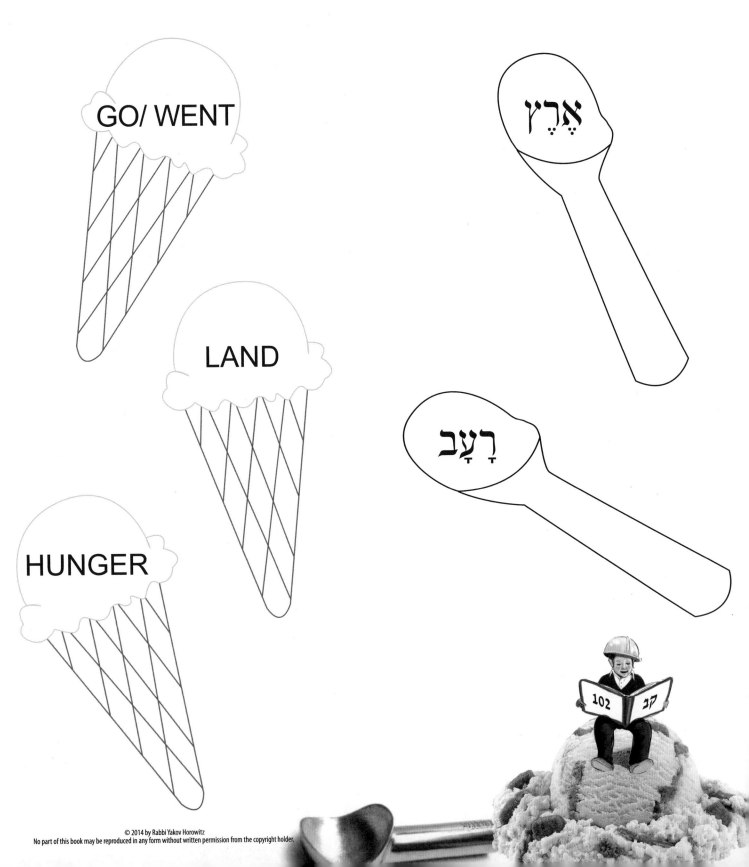

GO/ WENT

אֶרֶץ

LAND

רָעָב

HUNGER

And **there was**	וַיְהִי	
a hunger	רָעָב	רָעָב
in the land	בָּאָרֶץ	אֶרֶץ
and **he went down**	וַיֵּרֶד	
אַבְרָם	אַבְרָם	
to מִצְרַיִם	מִצְרַיְמָה	
to live	לָגוּר	
there	שָׁם	
because	כִּי	
it was heavy	כָבֵד	
the hunger	הָרָעָב	רָעָב
in the land	בָּאָרֶץ׃	אֶרֶץ

Color each prefix using the color chart below.

וַיְהִי בָּאָרֶץ

וַיֵּרֶד מִצְרַיְמָה בְּ

לָגוּר הָרָעָב

בָּאָרֶץ

COLOR CHART
AND = BLUE
THE = RED
FROM = GREEN
IN / WITH = ORANGE
TO / FOR = PINK
LIKE = PURPLE

1. Choose a color for each מִלָּה or שֹׁרֶשׁ on the left side of the page.

2. Color the שֹׁרֶשׁ or מִלָּה.

3. Color each word on the right side of the page using the same color as its מִלָּה or שֹׁרֶשׁ.

Color each שֹׁרֶשׁ or מִלָּה the same color as its meaning.
Some meanings will not be used.

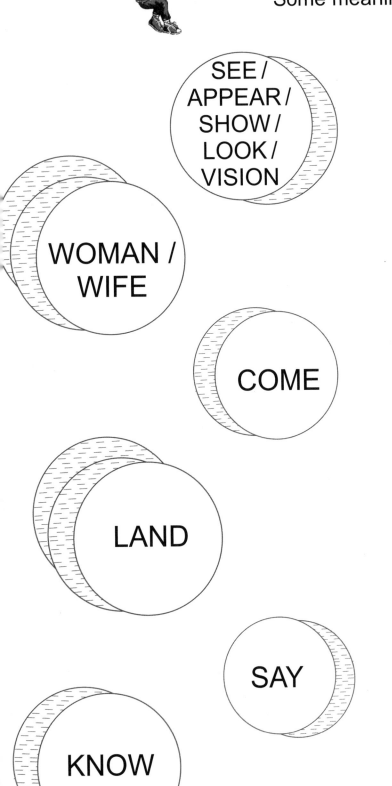

SEE /
APPEAR /
SHOW /
LOOK /
VISION

WOMAN /
WIFE

COME

LAND

SAY

KNOW

בוא

אמר

אִשָּׁה

ראה

יָדַע

And it was	וַיְהִי	
just as	כַּאֲשֶׁר	
he came closer	הִקְרִיב	
to come	לָבוֹא	בוא
to מִצְרַיִם	מִצְרָיְמָה	
and he said	וַיֹּאמֶר	אמר
to שָׂרַי	אֶל שָׂרַי	
his wife	אִשְׁתּוֹ	אשה
behold now	הִנֵּה נָא	
I know	יָדַעְתִּי	ידע
that	כִּי	
a woman of	אִשָּׁה	אשה
beautiful	יְפַת	
appearance	מַרְאֶה	ראה
you are	אָתְּ:	

Color each prefix using the color chart below.

וַיְהִי לְבוֹא

מִצְרַיְמָה

וַיֹּאמֶר

COLOR CHART
AND = BLUE
THE = RED
FROM = GREEN
IN / WITH = ORANGE
TO / FOR = PINK
LIKE = PURPLE

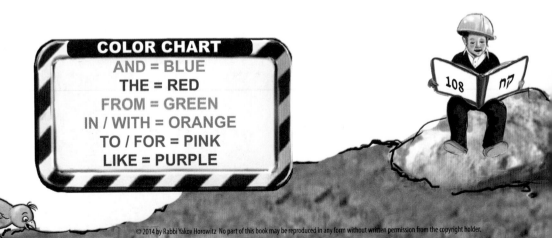

1. Choose a color for each מִלָה or שֹׁרֶשׁ on the left side of the page.

2. Color the שֹׁרֶשׁ or מִלָה.

3. Color each word on the right side of the page using the same color as its מִלָה or שֹׁרֶשׁ.

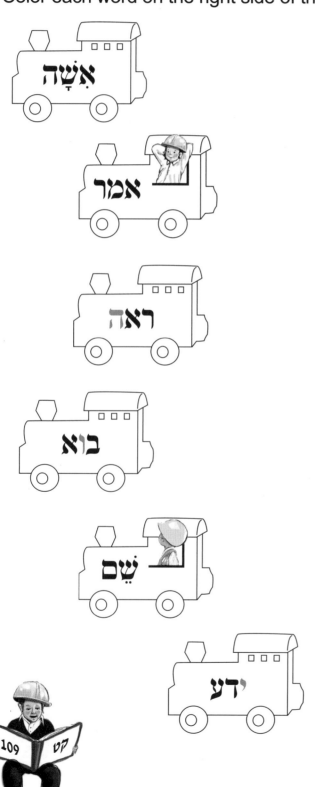

Color each שֹׁרֶשׁ or מִלָּה the same color as its meaning.
Some meanings will not be used.

WOMAN / WIFE

SAY

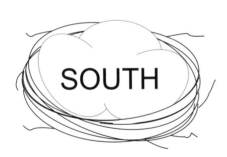

SOUTH

SEE / APPEAR / SHOW / LOOK / VISION

רָאָה

אָמַר

אִשָּׁה

110

And it will be	וְהָיָה
when	כִּי
they will see	יִרְאוּ
you	אֹתָךְ
the מִצְרִים	הַמִּצְרִים
and they will say	וְאָמְרוּ
"this is his wife"	אִשְׁתּוֹ זֹאת
and they will kill	וְהָרְגוּ
me	אֹתִי
and you	וְאֹתָךְ
they will let live	יְחַיּוּ:

ראה

אמר

אִשָּׁה

קי"א 111

Color each prefix using the color chart below.

וְהָיָה הֵמִצְרִים

וְאָמְרוּ וְהָרְגוּ

וְאֹתָךְ

COLOR CHART
AND = BLUE
THE = RED
FROM = GREEN
IN / WITH = ORANGE
TO / FOR = PINK
LIKE = PURPLE

112   קיב

1. Choose a color for each מִלָּה or שֹׁרֶשׁ on the left side of the page.

2. Color the מִלָּה or שֹׁרֶשׁ.

3. Color each word on the right side of the page using the same color as its מִלָּה or שֹׁרֶשׁ.

Color each שֹׁרֶשׁ or מִלָה the same color as its meaning.
Some meanings will not be used.

SOUL

WOMAN

SAY

SISTER

GOOD

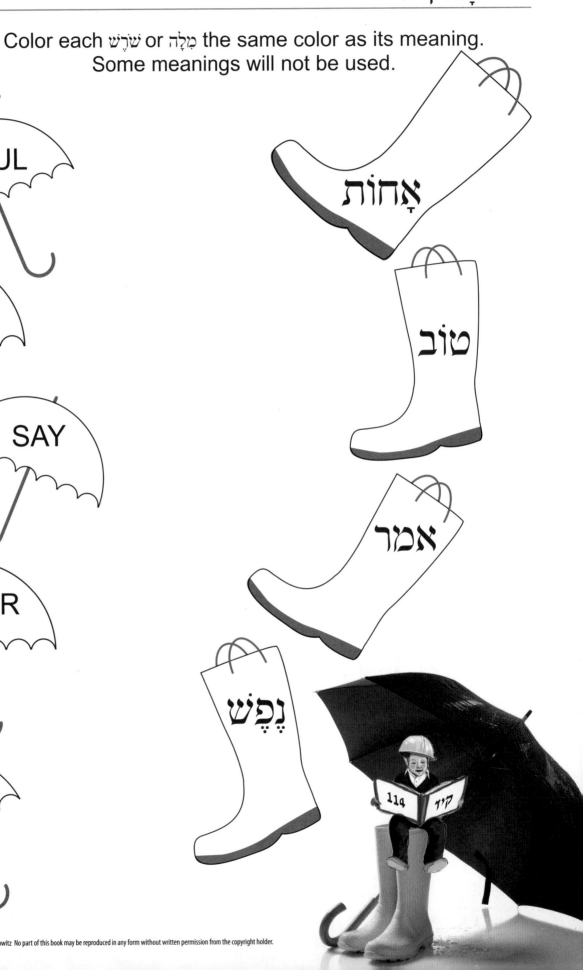

אָחוֹת

טוֹב

אמר

נֶפֶשׁ

Please say	אִמְרִי נָא	אמר
my sister	אֲחֹתִי	אָחוֹת
you are	אָתְּ	
so that	לְמַעַן	
it will be good	יִיטַב	טוב
for me	לִי	
through you	בַּעֲבוּרֵךְ	
and it will live	וְחָיְתָה	
my soul	נַפְשִׁי	נֶפֶשׁ
because of you	בִּגְלָלֵךְ:	

*שֶׁנֵּי

Color each prefix using the color chart below.

לִי

וְהָיְתָה

COLOR CHART

AND = BLUE
THE = RED
FROM = GREEN
IN / WITH = ORANGE
TO / FOR = PINK
LIKE = PURPLE

1. Choose a color for each מִלָּה or שֹׁרֶשׁ on the left side of the page.

2. Color the שֹׁרֶשׁ or מִלָּה.

3. Color each word on the right side of the page using the same color as its שֹׁרֶשׁ or מִלָּה.

Color each שֹׁרֶשׁ or מִלָּה the same color as its meaning.
Some meanings will not be used.

WOMAN /
WIFE

בּוֹא •

COME

רָאָה •

SEE /
APPEAR /
SHOW / LOOK /
VISION

• אִשָּׁה

SISTER

And **it was**	וַיְהִי	
when אַבְרָם came	כְּבוֹא אַבְרָם	בוא
to מִצְרַים	מִצְרָיְמָה	
and **they** saw	וַיִּרְאוּ	ראה
the מִצְרִים	הַמִּצְרִים	
the woman	אֶת הָאִשָּׁה	אִשָּׁה
that	כִּי	
beautiful	יָפָה	
she is	הִוא	
very	מְאֹד:	

Color each prefix using the color chart below.

וַיְהִי מִצְרַיְמָה

וַיִּרְאוּ

הַמִּצְרִים

הָאִשָּׁה

COLOR CHART

AND = BLUE
THE = RED
FROM = GREEN
IN / WITH = ORANGE
TO / FOR = PINK
LIKE = PURPLE

1. Choose a color for each מִלָה or שֹׁרֶשׁ on the left side of the page.

2. Color the שֹׁרֶשׁ or מִלָה.

3. Color each word on the right side of the page using the same color as its מִלָה or שֹׁרֶשׁ.

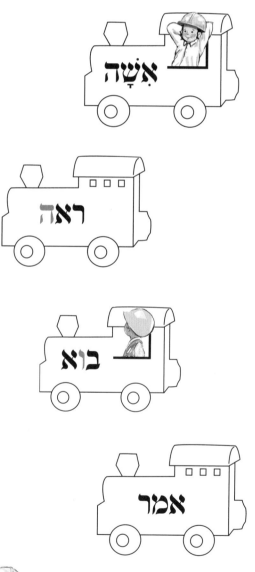

Color each שֹׁרֶשׁ or מִלָּה the same color as its meaning.
Some meanings will not be used.

TAKE

ראה

HOUSE

לקח

SAY

הלל

SEE / APPEAR /
SHOW / LOOK /
VISION

בַּיִת

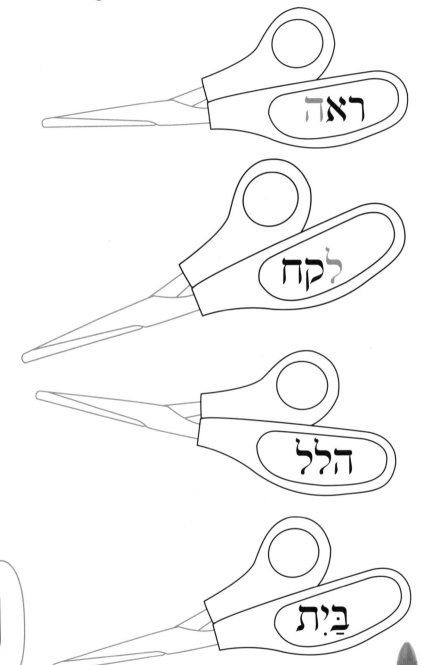

PRAISE

קכב   122

And they saw	וַיִּרְאוּ	**רֹאה**
her	אֹתָהּ	
the officers of	שָׂרֵי	
פַּרְעֹה	פַרְעֹה	
and they praised	וַיְהַלְלוּ	**הלל**
her	אֹתָהּ	
פַּרְעֹה to	אֶל פַּרְעֹה	
and she was taken	וַתֻּקַּח	**לקח**
the woman	הָאִשָּׁה	**אִשָּׁה**
to the house of	בֵּית	**בֵּית**
פַּרְעֹה	פַּרְעֹה:	

Color each prefix using the color chart below.

וַיִּרְאוּ

וַיְהַלְלוּ

וַתֻּקַּח הָאִשָּׁה

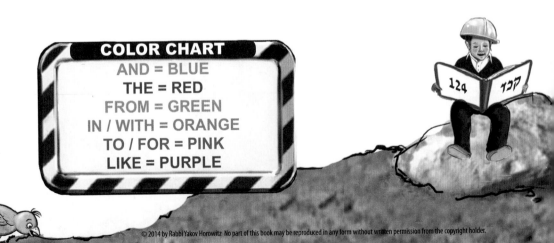

COLOR CHART
AND = BLUE
THE = RED
FROM = GREEN
IN / WITH = ORANGE
TO / FOR = PINK
LIKE = PURPLE

1. Choose a color for each מִלָּה or שֹׁרֶשׁ on the left side of the page.

2. Color the שֹׁרֶשׁ or מִלָּה.

3. Color each word on the right side of the page using the same color as its מִלָּה or שֹׁרֶשׁ.

לָקַח

בַּיִת

רָאָה

הִלֵּל

אָמַר

וַיְהַלְלוּ

וַתֻּקַּח

וַיִּרְאוּ

בֵּית

125

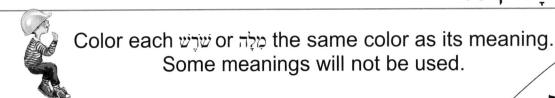

Color each שֹׁרֶשׁ or מִלָּה the same color as its meaning.
Some meanings will not be used.

שִׁפְחָה

עֶבֶד

טוֹב

GOOD

SISTER

SLAVE

MAID

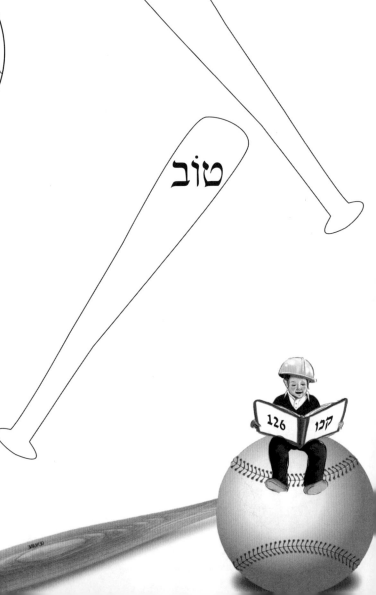

And to **אַבְרָם**	וּלְאַבְרָם	
he [פַּרְעֹה] did good	הֵיטִיב	**טוֹב**
because of her [שָׂרַי]	בַּעֲבוּרָהּ	
and there was	וַיְהִי	
to him	לוֹ	
sheep	צֹאן	
and cattle	וּבָקָר	
and male donkeys	וַחֲמֹרִים	
and slaves	וַעֲבָדִים	**עֶבֶד**
and maids	וּשְׁפָחֹת	**שִׁפְחָה**
and female donkeys	וַאֲתֹנֹת	
and camels	וּגְמַלִּים:	

Color each prefix using the color chart below.

וּלְאַבְרָם וַיְהִי לוֹ
צֹאן וּבָקָר וַחֲמֹרִים
וַעֲבָדִים וּשְׁפָחֹת
וַאֲתֹנֹת וּגְמַלִּים

COLOR CHART

AND = BLUE
THE = RED
FROM = GREEN
IN / WITH = ORANGE
TO / FOR = PINK
LIKE = PURPLE

128

קכח

1. Choose a color for each מִלָּה or שֹׁרֶשׁ on the left side of the page.

2. Color the שֹׁרֶשׁ or מִלָּה.

3. Color each word on the right side of the page using the same color as its מִלָּה or שֹׁרֶשׁ.

Color each שֹׁרֶשׁ or מִלָּה the same color as its meaning.
Some meanings will not be used.

גָּדֹל

נֶגַע

בַּיִת

אִשָּׁה

HOUSE

SERVANT

WOMAN /
WIFE

PLAGUE

BIG /
GREAT

130

And He plagued	וַיְנַגַּע
הַשֵּׁם	ה'
פַּרְעֹה	אֶת פַּרְעֹה
plagues	נְגָעִים
great	גְּדֹלִים
and his household	וְאֶת בֵּיתוֹ
because of the word of שָׂרַי	עַל דְּבַר שָׂרַי
the wife of	אֵשֶׁת
אַבְרָם	אַבְרָם:

נֶגַע

גָּדַל

בַּיִת

אִשָּׁה

Color each prefix using the color chart below.

COLOR CHART

AND = BLUE
THE = RED
FROM = GREEN
IN / WITH = ORANGE
TO / FOR = PINK
LIKE = PURPLE

1. Choose a color for each מִלָּה or שֹׁרֶשׁ on the left side of the page.

2. Color the שֹׁרֶשׁ or מִלָּה.

3. Color each word on the right side of the page using the same color as its מִלָּה or שֹׁרֶשׁ.

Color each שֹׁרֶשׁ or מִלָה the same color as its meaning.
Some meanings will not be used.

קרא

DO / MAKE

אמר

CALL

עשה

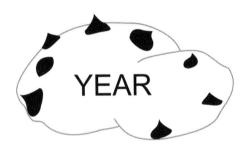
YEAR

SAY

אִשָׁה

WOMAN / WIFE

קרא	וַיִּקְרָא	And **he called**
	פַּרְעֹה	פַּרְעֹה
	לְאַבְרָם	אַבְרָם to
אמר	וַיֹּאמֶר	and **he said**
	מַה זֹּאת	what is this
עשה	עָשִׂיתָ	that **you have** done
	לִּי	to me
	לָמָה	why
	לֹא הִגַּדְתָּ	**did you not tell**
	לִּי	to me
	כִּי	that
אִשָּׁה	אִשְׁתְּךָ הִוא:	she is your wife

135 קלה

Color each prefix using the color chart below.

COLOR CHART
AND = BLUE
THE = RED
FROM = GREEN
IN / WITH = ORANGE
TO / FOR = PINK
LIKE = PURPLE

1. Choose a color for each מִלָּה or שֹׁרֶשׁ on the left side of the page.

2. Color the שֹׁרֶשׁ or מִלָּה.

3. Color each word on the right side of the page using the same color as its מִלָּה or שֹׁרֶשׁ.

Color each שֹׁרֶשׁ or מִלָּה the same color as its meaning.
Some meanings will not be used.

TAKE

GO / WENT

SISTER

SAY

WOMAN / WIFE

GOOD

אמר

אָחוֹת

לקח

הלך

אִשָּׁה

Why	לָמָה	
did you say	אָמַרְתָּ	אמר
"she is my sister"	אֲחֹתִי הִוא	אחות
and I took	וָאֶקַּח	לקח
her	אֹתָהּ	
to me	לִי	
for a wife	לְאִשָּׁה	אשה
and now	וְעַתָּה	
here is your wife	הִנֵּה אִשְׁתְּךָ	אשה
take (her)	קַח	לקח
and go	וָלֵךְ:	הלך

Color each prefix using the color chart below.

COLOR CHART
AND = BLUE
THE = RED
FROM = GREEN
IN / WITH = ORANGE
TO / FOR = PINK
LIKE = PURPLE

1. Choose a color for each מִלָה or שֹׁרֶשׁ on the left side of the page.

2. Color the שֹׁרֶשׁ or מִלָה.

3. Color each word on the right side of the page using the same color as its מִלָה or שֹׁרֶשׁ.

And he commanded	וַיְצַו
about him [אַבְרָם]	עָלָיו
פַּרְעֹה	פַּרְעֹה
men	אֲנָשִׁים
and they escorted	וַיְשַׁלְּחוּ
him	אֹתוֹ
and his wife	וְאֶת אִשְׁתּוֹ אִשָּׁה
and all	וְאֶת כָּל
that is to him	אֲשֶׁר לוֹ:

INTRODUCING

Prefix #7

א - I

rule:

Whenever there is an **א** prefix before a שֹׁרֶשׁ it means **I**.

 The **א** usually means **I will** (in the future) and can sometimes mean **I did** (in the past).

Examples of the **א** prefix:

I will bless - אֲבָרֵךְ

I will call - אֶקְרָא

I will go - אֵלֵךְ (שֹׁרֶשׁ ה-ל-כ)

Prefix Challenge!

An **א** before a שֹׁרֶשׁ means **"I will"** - in the future. However, if there is a וֹ (with a קָמֵץ) prefix before the **א**, the **א** will change to mean **"I did"** - in the past.

Example:
I will call - אֶקְרָא
and I called - וָאֶקְרָא

In the examples below there are 2 prefixes before the שֹׁרֶשׁ.

and I blessed - וָאֲבָרֵךְ

and I called - וָאֶקְרָא

and I went - וָאֵלֵךְ

143 · קמג

PREFIX א EXERCISE

Now it's your turn!
Add the missing prefix or prefixes to the שֹׁרֶשׁ.

I will bless - ‏___בָּרֵךְ .1

I will call - ‏___קְרָא .2

and I blessed - ‏___ ___בָּרֵךְ .3

and I called - ‏___ ___קְרָא .4

Draw a line from each prefix and שֹׁרֶשׁ to its meaning.

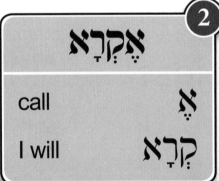

Write the number of the correct word on the line.

___make	עֲשֵׂה .1	___I will see	רְאֵה .1
___and I will make	אֶעֱשֶׂה .2	___see	אֶרְאֶה .2
___I will make	וְאֶעֱשֶׂה .3	___and I will see	וְאֶרְאֶה .3

 Some of the פְּסוּקִים that you have already learned in פָּרָשַׁת לֶךְ-לְךָ are below.

Circle the א prefixes that are found in each פָּסוּק. The red number before the פָּסוּק shows how many א prefixes you will need to find.

פָּסוּק א

(1) וַיֹּאמֶר ה' אֶל אַבְרָם לֶךְ לְךָ מֵאַרְצְךָ וּמִמּוֹלַדְתְּךָ
וּמִבֵּית אָבִיךָ אֶל הָאָרֶץ אֲשֶׁר אַרְאֶךָּ

פָּסוּק ב

(3) וְאֶעֶשְׂךָ לְגוֹי גָּדוֹל וַאֲבָרֶכְךָ וַאֲגַדְּלָה
שְׁמֶךָ וֶהְיֵה בְּרָכָה

פָּסוּק ג

(2) וַאֲבָרְכָה מְבָרְכֶיךָ וּמְקַלֶּלְךָ אָאֹר
וְנִבְרְכוּ בְךָ כֹּל מִשְׁפְּחֹת הָאֲדָמָה

INTRODUCING

Prefix #8

he - י

rule:

Whenever there is a י prefix before a שֹׁרֶשׁ it means **he**.

Did you know? The י usually means **he will** (in the future) but can sometimes mean **he did** (in the past). A י before a שֹׁרֶשׁ can also mean **they**. You will learn more about this at a later time!

Prefix Challenge!

A י before a שֹׁרֶשׁ means "he will" - in the future.

However, if there is a וַ (with a פַּתַח) prefix before the י, the י will change to mean "he did" - in the past.

Example:

he will say - יֹאמַר

and he said - וַיֹּאמֶר

Examples of the י prefix:

he will bless - יְבָרֵךְ

he will say - יֹאמַר

he will come - יָבוֹא

In the examples below there are 2 prefixes before the שֹׁרֶשׁ.

and he blessed -  וַיְבָרֶךְ

and he said - וַיֹּאמֶר

and he came - וַיָּבֹא

PREFIX י EXERCISE

Now it's your turn!
Add the missing prefix or prefixes to the שֹׁרֶשׁ.

he will **bless** - ___בָּרֵךְ .1

he will **say** - ___אָמַר .2

and he **blessed** - ___ ___בָּרֵךְ .3

and he **said** - ___ ___אָמַר .4

Draw a line from each prefix and שֹׁרֶשׁ to its meaning.

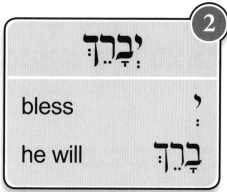

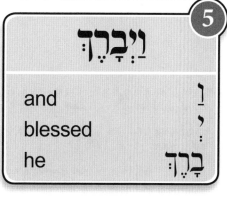

PREFIX י EXERCISE

Write the number of the correct word on the line.

___and he will see	רָאָה 1.	___he will make	עֹשֶׂה 1.
___see	יִרְאֶה 2.	___and he made	יַעֲשֶׂה 2.
___he will see	וְיִרְאֶה 3.	___make	וַיַּעֲשֶׂה 3.

Some of the פְּסוּקִים that you have already learned in פָּרָשַׁת לֶךְ-לְךָ are below.

Circle the י prefixes that are found in each פָּסוּק. The red number before the פָּסוּק shows how many י prefixes you will need to find.

פָּסוּק ד

(2) וַיֵּלֶךְ אַבְרָם כַּאֲשֶׁר דִּבֶּר אֵלָיו ה' וַיֵּלֶךְ אִתּוֹ לוֹט וְאַבְרָם בֶּן חָמֵשׁ שָׁנִים וְשִׁבְעִים שָׁנָה בְּצֵאתוֹ מֵחָרָן

פָּסוּק ו

(1) וַיַּעֲבֹר אַבְרָם בָּאָרֶץ עַד מְקוֹם שְׁכֶם עַד אֵלוֹן מוֹרֶה וְהַכְּנַעֲנִי אָז בָּאָרֶץ

פָּסוּק ז

Hint!
You will find the י prefixes before some שָׁרָשִׁים that you have learned!

(3) וַיֵּרָא ה' אֶל אַבְרָם וַיֹּאמֶר לְזַרְעֲךָ אֶתֵּן אֶת הָאָרֶץ הַזֹּאת וַיִּבֶן שָׁם מִזְבֵּחַ לַה' הַנִּרְאֶה אֵלָיו

קמח
148

פָּרָשַׁת

לֶךְ לְךָ

פֶּרֶק יג

And he **went up**	וַיַּעַל
אַבְרָם אַבְרָם	אַבְרָם
from מִצְרַיִם	מִמִּצְרַיִם
he	הוּא
and **his** wife	וְאִשְׁתּוֹ
and all	וְכָל
that was	אֲשֶׁר
to him	לוֹ
and **לוֹט**	וְלוֹט
with him	עִמּוֹ
to the **south**	הַנֶּגְבָּה:

אִשָּׁה

קנא 151

פָּסוּק א

1. Underline all the words that tell us where אַבְרָם is coming from.
2. Draw a box around the word that refers to שָׂרַי.
3. Circle all the words that refer to אַבְרָם's possesions.

וַיַּעַל אַבְרָם מִמִּצְרַיִם

הוּא וְאִשְׁתּוֹ וְכָל אֲשֶׁר

לוֹ וְלוֹט עִמּוֹ הַנֶּגְבָּה:

Color each prefix or suffix using the color chart below.

וַיַּעַל

מִמִּצְרַיִם

וְאִשְׁתּוֹ

וְלוֹ הַנֶּגְבָּה

COLOR CHART

AND = BLUE
THE = RED
FROM = GREEN
IN / WITH = ORANGE
TO / FOR = PINK
LIKE = PURPLE
HE = BROWN
I = GREY

153

קנג

And אַבְרָם (was)	וְאַבְרָם
heavy	כָּבֵד
very much	מְאֹד
with cattle	בַּמִּקְנֶה
with silver	בַּכֶּסֶף
and with gold	וּבַזָּהָב:

And he went	וַיֵּלֶךְ	הלך
on his traveling	לְמַסָּעָיו	נסע
from the south	מִנֶּגֶב	
and until	וְעַד	
(the city) בֵּית אֵל	בֵּית אֵל	
until	עַד	
the place	הַמָּקוֹם	
that	אֲשֶׁר	
was	הָיָה	
there	שָׁם	
his tent	אָהֳלֹה	אֹהֶל
in the beginning	בַּתְּחִלָּה	
between (the city) בֵּית אֵל	בֵּין בֵּית אֵל	
and between the (city) עָי	וּבֵין הָעָי:	

155

1. Draw a box around the word that
describes the action that אַבְרָם did.
2. Underline all the words that tell us where his tent was.

וַ...לֶךְ לְמַסָּעָיו מִנֶּגֶב וְעַד
בֵּית אֵל עַד הַמָּקוֹם אֲשֶׁר
הָיָה שָׁם אָהֳלֹה בַּתְּחִלָּה
בֵּין בֵּית אֵל וּבֵין הָעָי:

To the place of	אֶל מְקוֹם	
the מִזְבֵּחַ	הַמִּזְבֵּחַ	
that	אֲשֶׁר	
he made	עָשָׂה	עשה
there	שָׁם	
at first	בָּרִאשֹׁנָה	
and he called	וַיִּקְרָא	קרא
there	שָׁם	
אַבְרָם	אַבְרָם	
in the name of הַשֵּׁם	בְּשֵׁם ה'	שֵׁם

שְׁלִישִׁי

Color each שֹׁרֶשׁ or מִלָּה the same color as its meaning.
Some meanings will not be used.

TENT

HOUSE

CALL

TRAVEL

GO/
WENT

NAME

DO/
MAKE

Color each prefix using the color chart below.

וַיֵּלֶךְ

הַמָּקוֹם

בְּשֵׁם

וַיִּקְרָא

COLOR CHART

AND = BLUE
THE = RED
FROM = GREEN
IN / WITH = ORANGE
TO / FOR = PINK
LIKE = PURPLE
HE = BROWN
I = GREY

Color each שֹׁרֶשׁ or מִלָּה the same color as its meaning.
Some meanings will not be used.

GO/ WENT

CALL

SIT/ LIVE

TENT

LAND

POSSESSION

יָשַׁב

אֹהֶל

אֶרֶץ

הָלַךְ

רְכוּשׁ

160

And **also**	וְגַם	
to לוֹט	לְלוֹט	
who went	הַהֹלֵךְ	**הלך**
with אַבְרָם	אֶת אַבְרָם	
there was	הָיָה	
sheep	צֹאן	
and **cattle**	וּבָקָר	
and **tent**s	וְאֹהָלִים:	**אֹהֶל**

Color each prefix using the color chart below.

וְגַם לְלוֹט

וּבָקָר

וְאֹהָלִים

COLOR CHART

AND = BLUE
THE = RED
FROM = GREEN
IN / WITH = ORANGE
TO / FOR = PINK
LIKE = PURPLE
HE = BROWN
I = GREY

And it could not support	וְלֹא נָשָׂא	נשא
them	אֹתָם	
the land	הָאָרֶץ	אֶרֶץ
to live	לָשֶׁבֶת	ישב
together	יַחְדָּו	
because	כִּי	
it was	הָיָה	
their possessions	רְכוּשָׁם	רְכוּשׁ
were many	רָב	
and they were not able	וְלֹא יָכְלוּ	
to live	לָשֶׁבֶת	ישב
together	יַחְדָּו:	

163

1. Choose a color for each מִלָה or שֹׁרֶשׁ on the left side of the page.

2. Color the שֹׁרֶשׁ or מִלָה.

3. Color each word on the right side of the page using the same color as its מִלָה or שֹׁרֶשׁ.

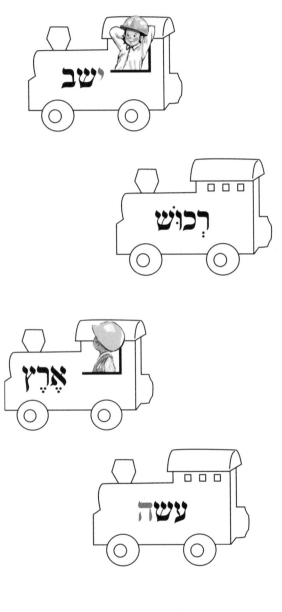

And there was	וַיְהִי	
an argument	רִיב	
between	בֵּין	
the shepherds of	רֹעֵי	רֹעֶה
the cattle of אַבְרָם	מִקְנֵה אַבְרָם	
and between	וּבֵין	
the shepherds of	רֹעֵי	רֹעֶה
the cattle of לוֹט	מִקְנֵה לוֹט	
and the כְּנַעֲנִי	וְהַכְּנַעֲנִי	
and the פְּרִזִּי	וְהַפְּרִזִּי	
then lived	אָז יֹשֵׁב	יָשַׁב
in the land	בָּאָרֶץ:	אֶרֶץ

Color each שֹׁרֶשׁ or מִלָה the same color as its meaning.
Some meanings will not be used.

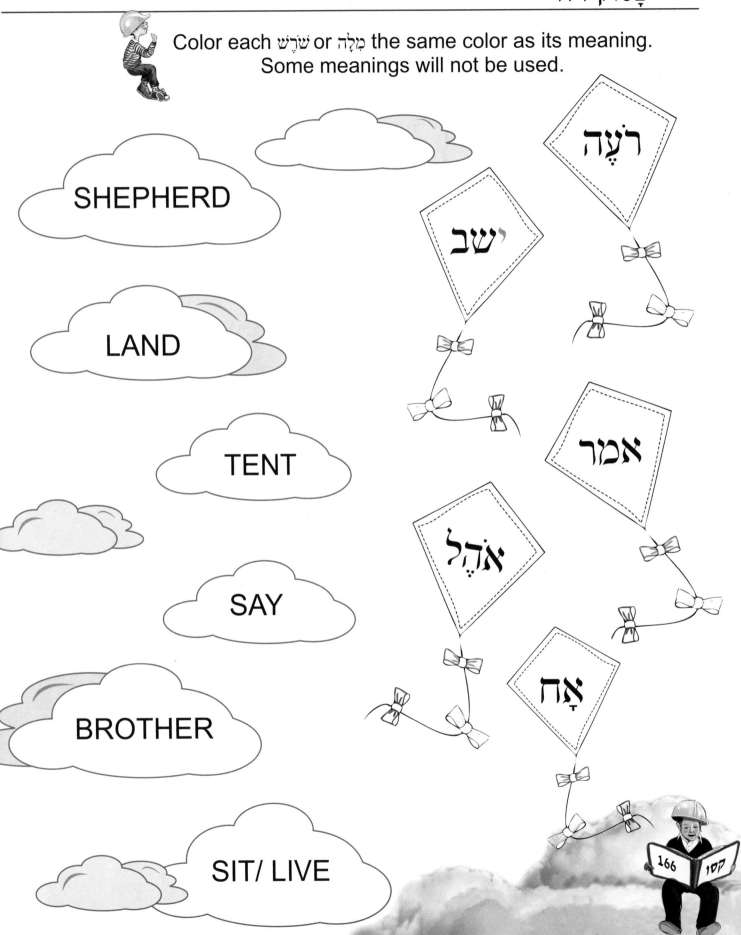

SHEPHERD

LAND

TENT

SAY

BROTHER

SIT/ LIVE

רֹעֶה

יֹשֵׁב

אָמַר

אֹהֶל

אָח

אמר	וַיֹּאמֶר	And he said
	אַבְרָם	אַבְרָם Avram
	אֶל לוֹט	to לוֹט
	אַל נָא תְהִי	please let there not be
	מְרִיבָה	an argument
	בֵּינִי	between me
	וּבֵינֶךָ	and between you
	וּבֵין	and between
רֹעֶה	רֹעַי	my shepherds
	וּבֵין	and between
רֹעֶה	רֹעֶיךָ	your shepherds
	כִּי	because
	אֲנָשִׁים	men
אָח	אַחִים	brothers (relatives)
	אֲנַחְנוּ:	we are

פָּסוּק ח

1. <u>Underline</u> all the words that אַבְרָם is saying.

2. Draw a box around the words that tell us that אַבְרָם and לוֹט are relatives.

3. Circle all the words that translate, "between".

וַיֹּאמֶר אַבְרָם אֶל לוֹט

אַל נָא תְהִי מְרִיבָה בֵּינִי

וּבֵינֶךָ וּבֵין רֹעַי וּבֵין רֹעֶיךָ

כִּי אֲנָשִׁים אַחִים אֲנָחְנוּ׃

Is not	הֲלֹא
the entire land	כָל הָאָרֶץ
before you	לְפָנֶיךָ
please separate	הִפָּרֶד נָא
from me	מֵעָלָי
if	אִם
(you go to) the left	הַשְּׂמֹאל
and I will (go) to the right	וְאֵימִנָה
and if	וְאִם
(you go to) the right	הַיָּמִין
and I will (go) to the left	וְאַשְׂמְאִילָה:

אֶרֶץ

פָּסוּק ט

1. <u>Underline</u> all the words that אַבְרָם is saying.
2. Draw a box around the letters that translate, "I will".
3. Circle all the words that have the translation "right".

הֲלֹא כָל הָאָרֶץ לְפָנֶיךָ

הִפָּרֶד נָא מֵעָלָי אִם

הַשְּׂמֹאל וְאֵימִנָה וְאִם

הַיָּמִין וְאַשְׂמְאִילָה׃

And he raised	וַיִּשָּׂא	נשא
	לוֹט	
his eyes	אֶת עֵינָיו	עַיִן
and he saw	וַיַּרְא	ראה
the entire plain	אֶת כָּל כִּכַּר	
of the יַרְדֵּן	הַיַּרְדֵּן	
that	כִּי	
it is all	כֻלָּהּ	
watered	מַשְׁקֶה	
before	לִפְנֵי	
הַשֵּׁם destroyed	שַׁחֵת ה'	
סְדוֹם and עֲמֹרָה	אֶת סְדֹם וְאֶת עֲמֹרָה	
like the garden of	כְּגַן	
הַשֵּׁם	ה'	
like the land מִצְרַיִם	כְּאֶרֶץ מִצְרַיִם	אֶרֶץ
coming to	בֹּאֲכָה	בוא
	צֹעַר׃ צֹעַר	

פָּסוּק י

1. Underline all the words that are names of places.
2. Draw a box around the words that describe כִּכַּר הַיַּרְדֵּן.
3. Circle all the words that tell what לוֹט did with his eyes.

וַיִּשָּׂא לוֹט אֶת עֵינָיו וַיַּרְא אֶת

כָּל כִּכַּר הַיַּרְדֵּן כִּי כֻלָּהּ מַשְׁקֶה

לִפְנֵי שַׁחֵת ה' אֶת סְדֹם וְאֶת

עֲמֹרָה כְּגַן ה' כְּאֶרֶץ מִצְרַיִם

בֹּאֲכָה צֹעַר:

And he **chose**	וַיִּבְחַר	
for **himself**	לוֹ	
לוֹט	לוֹט	
the entire plain	אֵת כָּל כִּכַּר	
of the יַרְדֵן	הַיַּרְדֵן	
and he **traveled**	וַיִּסַּע	**נסע**
לוֹט	לוֹט	
from **the east**	מִקֶּדֶם	
and **they separated**	וַיִּפָּרְדוּ	
a man	אִישׁ	
from **near**	מֵעַל	
his brother	אָחִיו:	**אָח**

Color each שֹׁרֶשׁ or מִלָה the same color as its meaning.
Some meanings will not be used.

BROTHER

EYE

COME

SEE/
APPEAR/SHOW/
LOOK/VISION

TENT

GO/
WENT

TRAVEL

בוֹא

נָסַע

אָח

אֹהֶל

רָאָה

עַיִן

174 קעד

פָּסוּק יא

1. <u>Underline</u> the place that לוֹט chose.

2. Draw a box around the word that describes where לוֹט traveled fro

3. Circle all the words that describe אַבְרָם and לוֹט.

וַיִּבְחַר לוֹ לוֹט אֵת כָּל כִּכַּר
הַיַּרְדֵּן וַיִּסַּע לוֹט מִקֶּדֶם
וַיִּפָּרְדוּ אִישׁ מֵעַל אָחִיו:

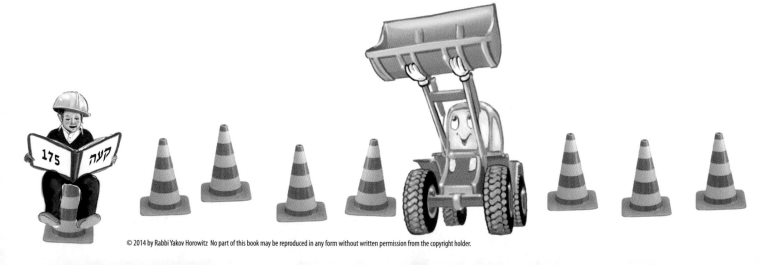

Color each prefix using the color chart below.

וַיִּבְחַר לוֹ וַיִּסַּע

מִקֶּדֶם מֵעַל

COLOR CHART

AND = BLUE
THE = RED
FROM = GREEN
IN / WITH = ORANGE
TO / FOR = PINK
LIKE = PURPLE
HE = BROWN
I = GREY

	אַבְרָם	אַבְרָם
ישׁב	יָשַׁב	lived
אֶרֶץ	בְּאֶרֶץ כְּנַעַן	in the land כְּנַעַן
	וְלוֹט	and לוֹט
ישׁב	יָשַׁב	lived
	בְּעָרֵי	in the cities of
	הַכִּכָּר	the plain
	וַיֶּאֱהַל	and he pitched tents
	עַד	until
	סְדֹם:	סְדֹם

פָּסוּק יב

1. <u>Underline</u> all the words that are names of people.
2. Draw a box around the name of the place where אַבְרָם lived.
3. Circle the name of the place where לוֹט lived.

אַבְרָם יָשַׁב בְּאֶרֶץ

כְּנַעַן וְלוֹט יָשַׁב בְּעָרֵי

הַכִּכָּר וַיֶּאֱהַל עַד

סְדֹם:

And the people of	וְאַנְשֵׁי
of Sdom	סְדֹם
were bad	רָעִים
and sinful	וְחַטָּאִים
to Hashem	לַה'
very much	מְאֹד:

Color each שֹׁרֶשׁ or מִלָּה the same color as its meaning.
Some meanings will not be used.

RAISE

אמר

SHEPHERD

נשא

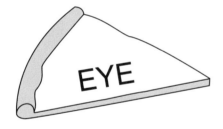

EYE

עַיִן

SAY

ראה

SEE /
APPEAR / SHOW /
LOOK / VISION

קף 180

And **הַשֵּׁם**	וַה'	
said	אָמַר	**אמר**
אַבְרָם to	אֶל אַבְרָם	
after	אַחֲרֵי	
לוֹט separated	הִפָּרֶד לוֹט	
from him	מֵעִמּוֹ	
raise now	שָׂא נָא	**נשא**
your eyes	עֵינֶיךָ	**עַיִן**
and look	וּרְאֵה	**ראה**
from the place	מִן הַמָּקוֹם	
that	אֲשֶׁר	
you are there	אַתָּה שָׁם	
to the north	צָפֹנָה	
and to the south	וָנֶגְבָּה	
and to the east	וָקֵדְמָה	
and to the west	וָיָמָּה:	

קפא 181

פָּסוּק יד

1. Underline all the words that הַשֵׁם said.
2. Draw a box around each word that tells a direction.
3. Circle the name of the person to whom הַשֵׁם is talking.

וַה' אָמַר אֶל אַבְרָם אַחֲרֵי
הִפָּרֶד לוֹט מֵעִמּוֹ שָׂא נָא
עֵינֶיךָ וּרְאֵה מִן הַמָּקוֹם
אֲשֶׁר אַתָּה שָׁם צָפֹנָה וָנֶגְבָּה
וָקֵדְמָה וָיָמָּה:

English	Hebrew	Root
Because	כִּי	
the entire land	אֶת כָּל הָאָרֶץ	אֶרֶץ
that	אֲשֶׁר	
you	אַתָּה	
see	רֹאֶה	רֹאֶה
to you	לְךָ	
I will give it	אֶתְּנֶנָּה	נתן
and to your children	וּלְזַרְעֲךָ	זֶרַע
forever	עַד עוֹלָם:	

פָּסוּק טו

Color each שֹׁרֶשׁ or מִלָּה the same color as its meaning.

GIVE

אֶרֶץ

רָאָה

SEE / APPEAR /
SHOW /
LOOK / VISION

נתנ

LAND

זֶרַע

CHILDREN

פָּסוּק טו

1. <u>Underline</u> all the words that הַשֵּׁם is saying.
2. Draw a box around the word that refers to אֶרֶץ יִשְׂרָאֵל.
3. Circle all the words that refer to בְּנֵי יִשְׂרָאֵל.
4. Draw a triangle around the words that refers to אַבְרָם.

כִּי אֶת כָּל הָאָרֶץ

אֲשֶׁר אַתָּה רֹאֶה לְךָ

אֶתְּנֶנָּה וּלְזַרְעֲךָ עַד

עוֹלָם:

Color each שֹׁרֶשׁ or מִלָּה the same color as its meaning.
Some meanings will not be used.

GIVE

זֶרַע

LAND

אֶרֶץ

GO/ WENT

הלכ

TENT

נתנ

CHILDREN

And **I will make**	וְשַׂמְתִּי	
your children	אֶת זַרְעֲךָ	זֶרַע
like the **dust of**	כַּעֲפַר	
the land	הָאָרֶץ	אֶרֶץ
that	אֲשֶׁר	
if	אִם	
he **will be able**	יוּכַל	
a man	אִישׁ	
to **count**	לִמְנוֹת	
the dust of	אֶת עֲפַר	
the land	הָאָרֶץ	אֶרֶץ
also your children	גַּם זַרְעֲךָ	זֶרַע
will be counted	יִמָּנֶה:	

פָּסוּק טז

1. Underline all the words that הַשֵׁם is saying.
2. Draw a box around each word that הַשֵׁם is comparing the בְּנֵי יִשְׂרָאֵל to.
3. Circle all the words that refer to **you**!

וְשַׂמְתִּי אֶת זַרְעֲךָ כַּעֲפַר

הָאָרֶץ אֲשֶׁר אִם יוּכַל

אִישׁ לִמְנוֹת אֶת עֲפַר

הָאָרֶץ גַּם זַרְעֲךָ יִמָּנֶה:

Get up	קוּם	
go	הִתְהַלֵּךְ	**הלך**
in the land	בָּאָרֶץ	**אֶרֶץ**
to its length	לְאׇרְכָּהּ	
and to its width	וּלְרׇחְבָּהּ	
because	כִּי	
to you	לְךָ	
I will give it	אֶתְּנֶנָּה:	**נתן**

פָּסוּק יז

1. <u>Underline</u> all the words that הַשֵׁם is saying.

2. Draw a box around the word that refers to אֶרֶץ יִשְׂרָאֵל.

3. Draw a triangle around the word that refers to אַבְרָם.

קוּם הִתְהַלֵּךְ בָּאָרֶץ לְאָרְכָּהּ וּלְרָחְבָּהּ כִּי לְךָ אֶתְּנֶנָּה:

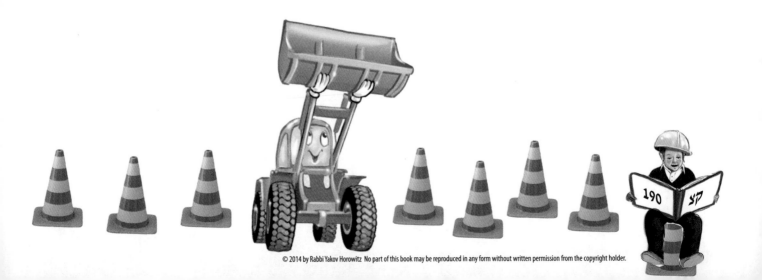

And he **pitched tents**	וַיֶּאֱהַל	
אַבְרָם	אַבְרָם	
and he **came**	וַיָּבֹא	**בוא**
and he **lived**	וַיֵּשֶׁב	**ישב**
in the plains of מַמְרֵא	בְּאֵלֹנֵי מַמְרֵא	
that is	אֲשֶׁר	
חֶבְרוֹן in	בְּחֶבְרוֹן	
and he **built**	וַיִּבֶן	
there	שָׁם	
a מִזְבֵּחַ	מִזְבֵּחַ	
הַשֵּׁם to	לַה׳:	

רְבִיעִי

פָּסוּק יח

1. Draw a box around the city where אַבְרָם lived.
2. Underline all the action words in this פָּסוּק.

וַיֶּאֱהַל אַבְרָם וַיָּבֹא וַיֵּשֶׁב
בְּאֵלֹנֵי מַמְרֵא אֲשֶׁר בְּחֶבְרוֹן
וַיִּבֶן שָׁם מִזְבֵּחַ לַה׳:

קצב 192

צִיצִת

אֶזְרֹן

אָבִיב

בִּשְׁוָן

זָיִן

34
SHEPHERD

32
LIVE/SIT

35
EYE
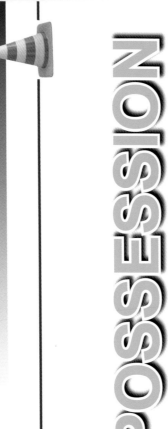

33
POSSESSION

31
RAISE/SUPPORT

26

נֶגֶד

28

וְהַשְׁכֵּם

30

יָרַד

25

בֹּקֶר

27

הֵיכָל

29

אֶשֶׁב

BIG / GREAT

MAID

PRAISE

PLAGUE

SLAVE

GOOD

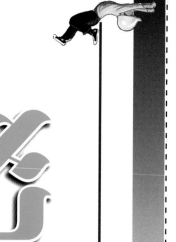
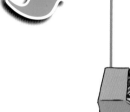

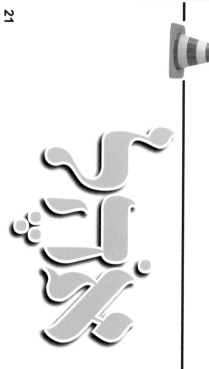

20

22

24

19

21

23

KNOW

24

CALL

22

MOUNTAIN

20

TRAVEL

23

TENT

21

GIVE

19

גּוֹי

סַע

אָדֶה

סָל

שְׁנִי

אִצְדָּה

CHILDREN

18

COME

16

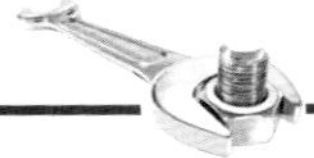

BROTHER

14

PASS

17

SOUL

15

WOMAN / WIFE

13

TAKE

YEAR

BLESS

GO OUT

FAMILY

NAME

DO/
MAKE

6

HOUSE/
HOUSEHOLD

4

GO/
WENT

2

SEE/ APPEAR/
SHOW/ LOOK/
VISION

5

LAND

3

SAY

1

like

to/for

in/with

and

from

the